All for STRINGS

THEORY WORKBOOK 2
by Gerald E. Anderson and Robert S. Frost

Dear String Student:
Welcome to **ALL FOR STRINGS-THEORY WORKBOOK 2**.

With the successful completion of THEORY WORKBOOK 1 you have learned much about the fundamentals and theory of music. THEORY WORKBOOK 2 builds upon the foundation you have already established and introduces you to many new musical concepts.

We hope that by using this workbook as a companion to ALL FOR STRINGS-Book 2 you will increase your musical understanding as you build your performance skills.

Best Wishes!

Gerald E. Anderson
Robert S. Frost

ISBN 0-8497-3253-0

KJOS NEIL A. KJOS MUSIC COMPANY • SAN DIEGO, CALIFORNIA

1. MATCHING

Match the correct definition to the word or symbol. Write the letter of the correct definition on the blank provided.

1. _______ **Allegro**

2. _______ **Andante**

3. _______ **Moderato**

4. _______ Arco

5. _______ L. H.

6. _______ Tie

7. _______ ⊕

8. _______ *Da Capo*

9. _______ Slur

10. _______ Pizzicato

11. _______ M.

12. _______ 𝄐

13. _______ W. B.

14. _______ 𝄋

15. _______ *Dal Segno*

16. _______ ,

17. _______ *rit.*

18. _______ U. H.

19. _______ Solo

20. _______ *Fine*

21. _______ Ensemble

22. _______ *divisi*

a. moderately slow

b. pluck the string

c. coda sign

d. play with a full bow

e. moderate speed

f. part of the section plays the top note; part plays the bottom note

g. play in the upper half of the bow

h. fermata

i. quick and lively

j. play with the bow

k. go back to the sign

l. a curved line that connects notes of the same pitch

m. go back to the beginning

n. a group usually playing different parts

o. play in the middle of the bow

p. play in the lower half of the bow

q. a curved line to indicate notes to be played smoothly in one bow

r. Dal Segno sign

s. finish or end

t. bow lift

u. one person plays

v. gradually slow the tempo

2. NAME NOTES

Write the name of the note on the blank provided.

__ __ __ __ __ __ __ __ __ __ __ __ __ __ __ __

3. MUSICAL MATH

Fill in each blank with the number that solves each musical math problem.

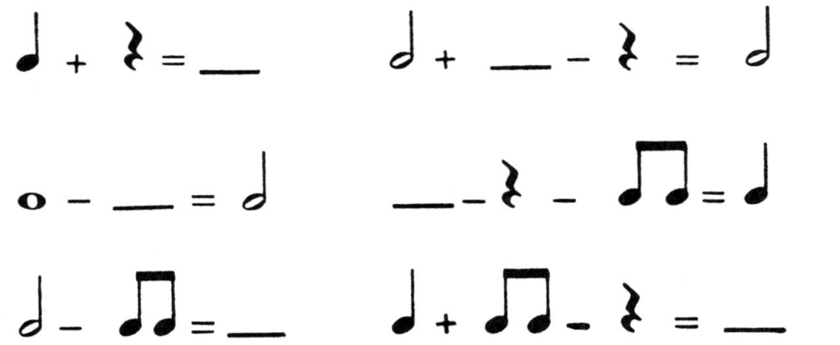
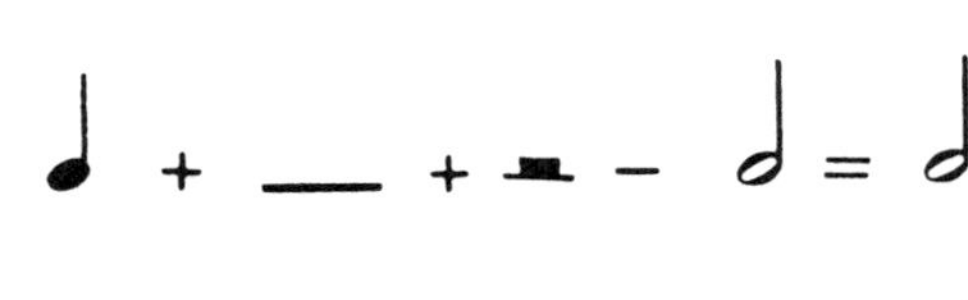

4. DRAW BAR LINES/WRITE COUNTING

Draw bar lines for the three lines of music below so that each measure contains the correct number of beats. Write the counting on the blanks provided.

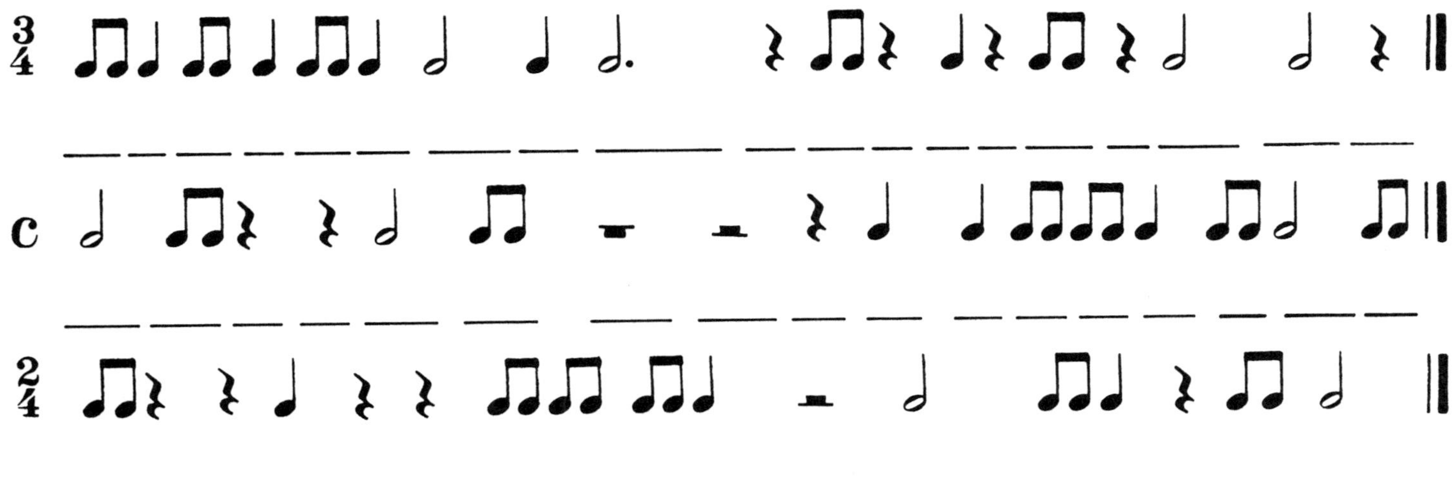

5. IDENTIFY SLURS AND TIES

Write a **T** under all the ties and an **S** under all the slurs.

6. BALANCE THE SCALE

Write ONE note to balance each scale.

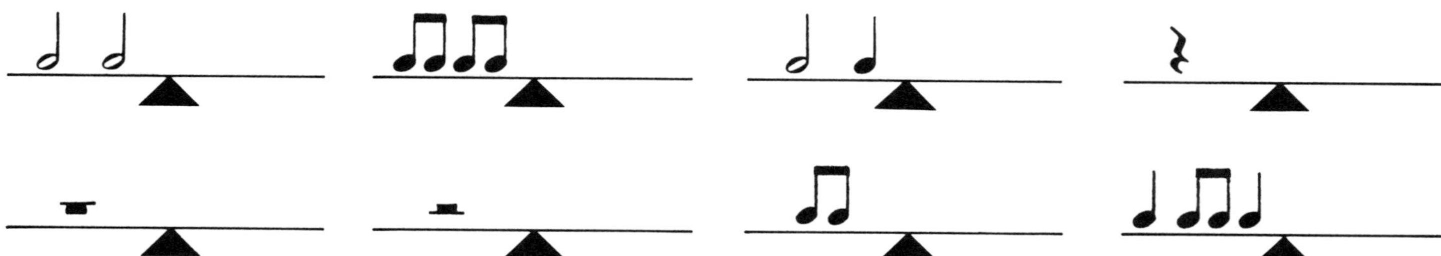

7. CONSTRUCT SCALES/KEY SIGNATURES/TETRACHORDS

1. Draw your clef and the correct key signature for each scale.
2. Construct the Major scales as requested. Use whole notes.
3. Mark both half steps included in each scale.
4. Circle the lower and upper tetrachords of each scale.

C Major

G Major

D Major

8. LEARN FLATS

A flat lowers a note by one half step. See the keyboard below:

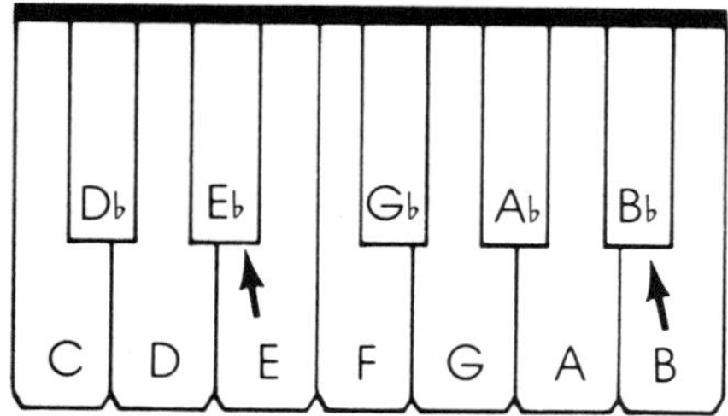

9. DRAW FLAT SIGNS

① Trace then draw several flat signs on different lines and spaces.
② Draw the notes with flats as requested. Use quarter or half notes. Be sure each stem points in the correct direction.

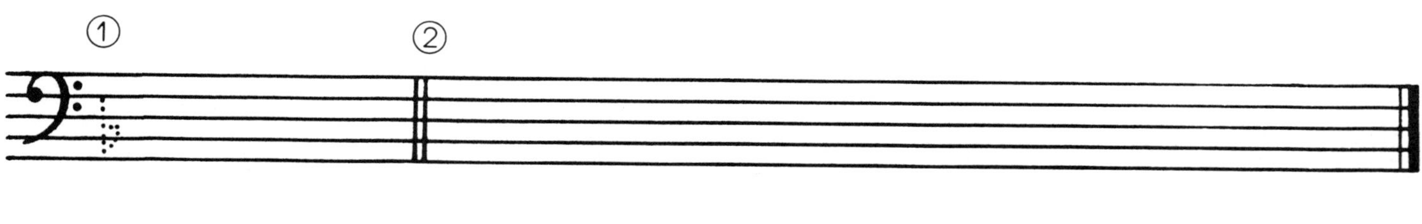

10. FINGERING CHART

Write the name of the note that is played at the place of each circle and square on the fingering chart below.

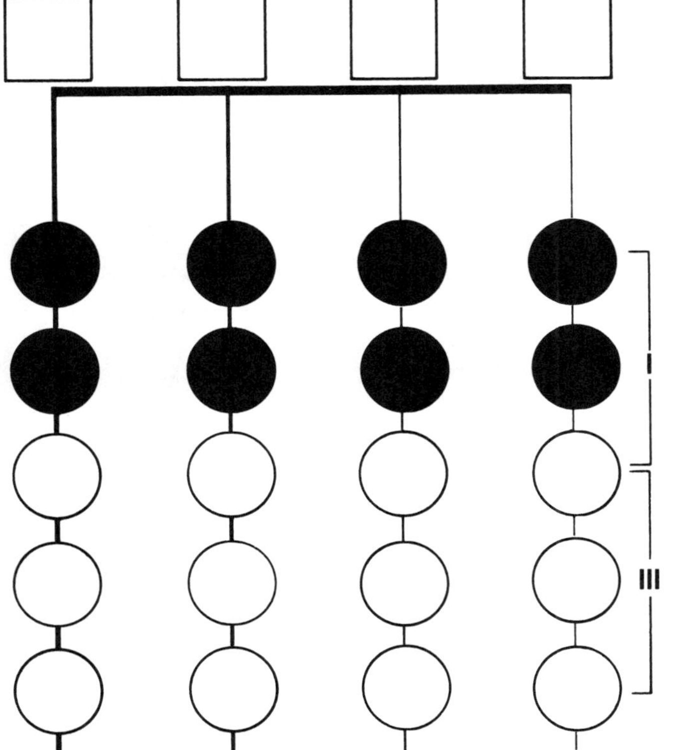

Questions.

G to A is a _______________ step.

C to D♭ is a _______________ step.

B♭ to B♮ is a _______________ step.

G to A♭ is a _______________ step.

A to B is a _______________ step.

D to E♭ is a _______________ step.

C to D is a _______________ step.

A to B♭ is a _______________ step.

11. NAME NOTES/DRAW NOTES

① Write the name of each note on the blank provided. ② Draw the notes from the fingering chart above on the staff as requested. Use half notes. Be sure each stem points in the correct direction.

12. KEYBOARD STUDY

Write the letters on the keys for all the notes shown in the fingering chart above. Show proper relationship to middle C.

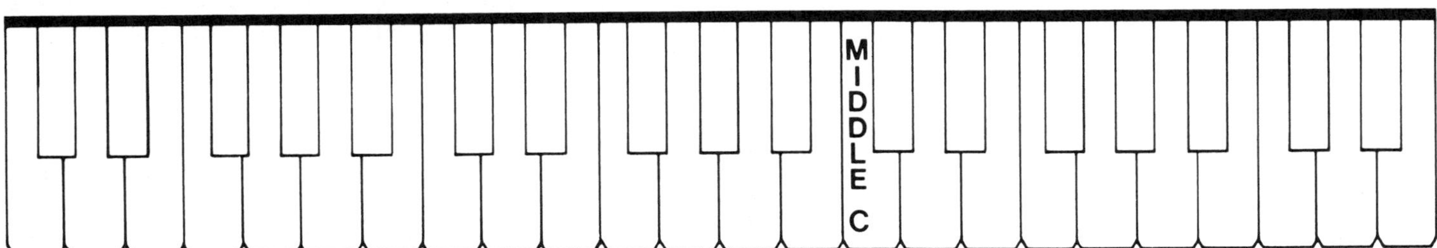

13. FINGERING CHART

Write the name of the note that is played at the place of each circle and square on the fingering chart below.

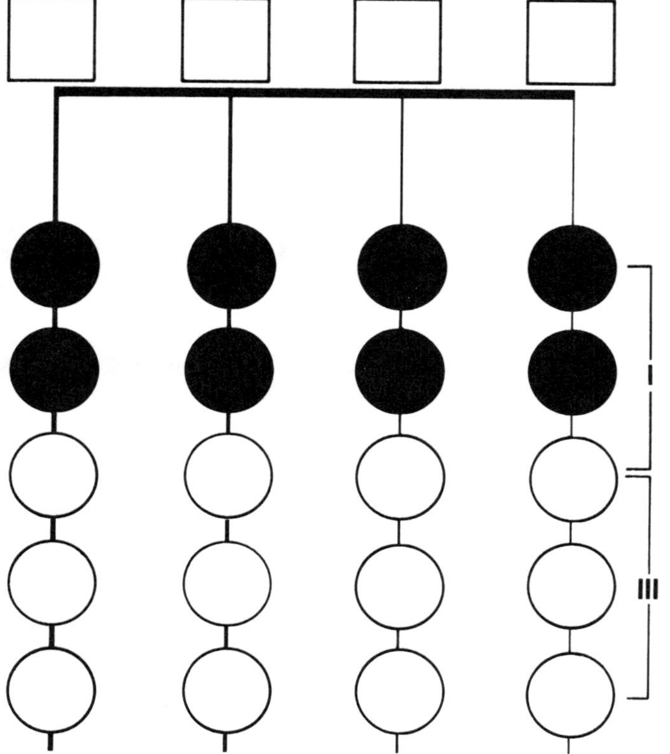

Questions:

A♯ to B is a _______________ step.

C to D is a _______________ step.

D to D♯ is a _______________ step.

G to A is a _______________ step.

C♯ to D is a _______________ step.

D to E is a _______________ step.

G♯ to A is a _______________ step.

A to B is a _______________ step.

14. NAME NOTES/DRAW NOTES

①Write the name of each note on the blank provided. ② Draw the notes from the fingering chart above on the staff as requested. Use quarter notes. Be sure each stem points in the correct direction.

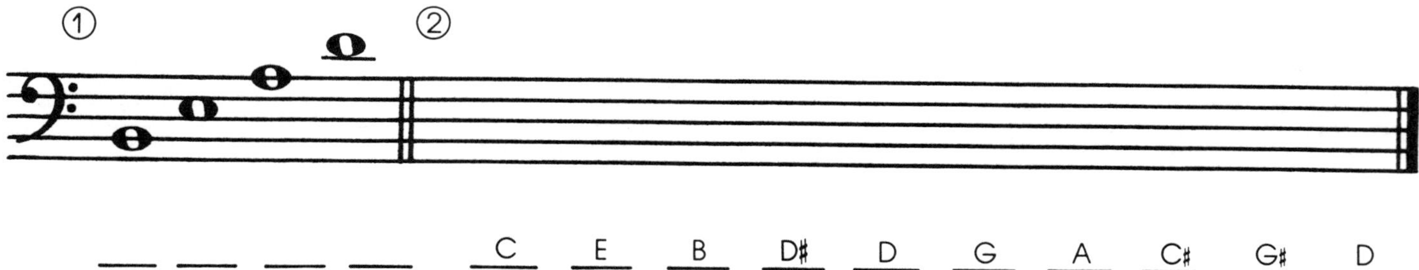

15. KEYBOARD STUDY

Write the letters on the keys for all the notes shown in the fingering chart above. Show proper relationship to middle C.

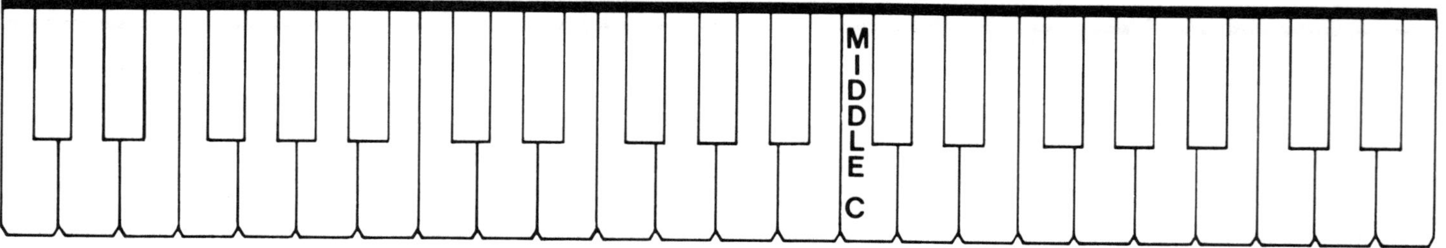

16. IDENTIFY KEY SIGNATURES

Write the letter name of the key on the blank provided. Place the tonic note (key note) on the staff.
Use whole notes.

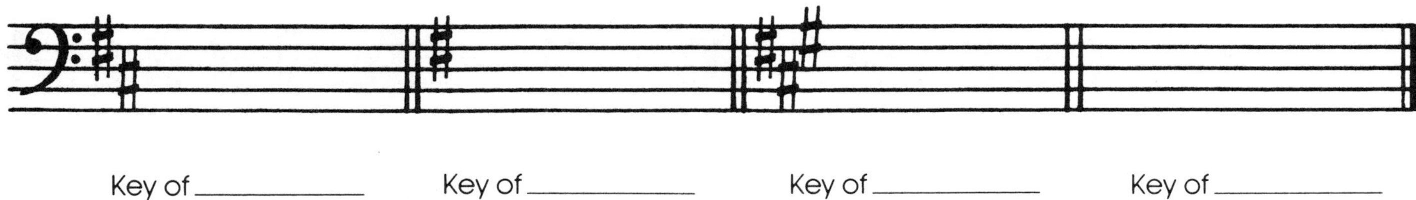

Key of ___________   Key of ___________   Key of ___________   Key of ___________

17. IDENTIFY HIGH AND LOW NOTES

Identify the fingering for each of the notes in 1st position as follows: On the blanks provided, place a **4** for notes played with a fourth finger and a **2** for notes played with a second finger.

___ ___ ___   ___ ___ ___   ___ ___ ___   ___ ___ ___

18. MUSICAL MATH

Solve each musical math problem by placing the number of the correct answer above each division line.

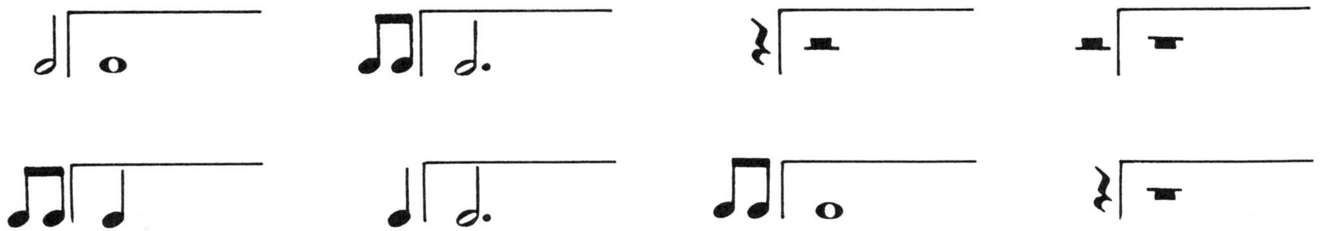

19. NAME INTERVALS

Write the size of each interval on the blank provided. e.g. 2nd, 3rd.

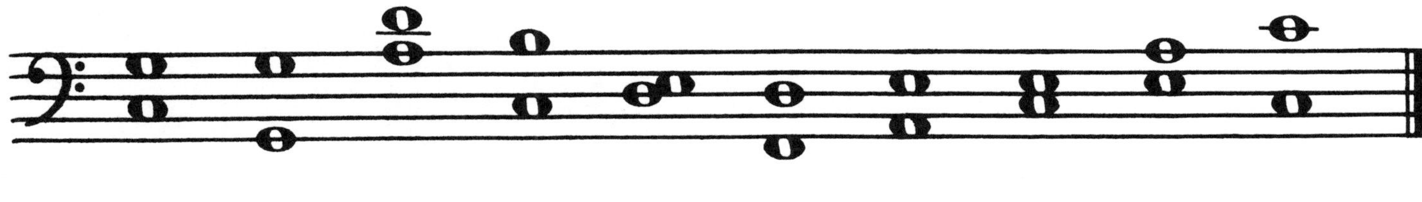

___ ___ ___ ___ ___ ___ ___

20. CONSTRUCT INTERVALS

Construct the interval ABOVE each written note as requested. Use whole notes.

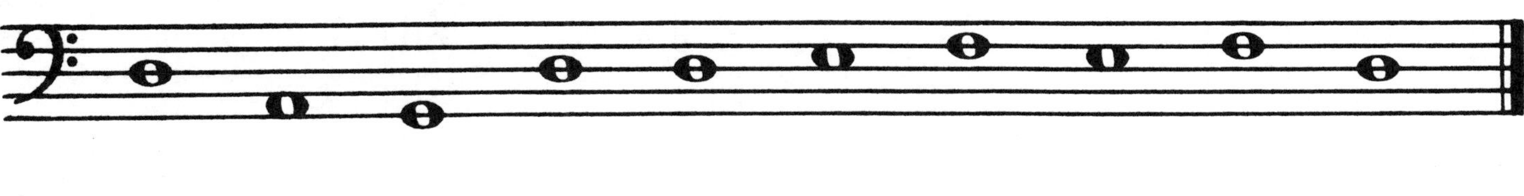

5th   3rd   Octave   7th   2nd   Unison   4th   6th   5th   Octave

21. DRAW BAR LINES/WRITE COUNTING

Draw bar lines for the three lines of music below so that each measure contains the correct number of beats. Write the counting on the blanks provided.

22. BALANCE THE SCALE

Write ONE note or rest to balance each scale.

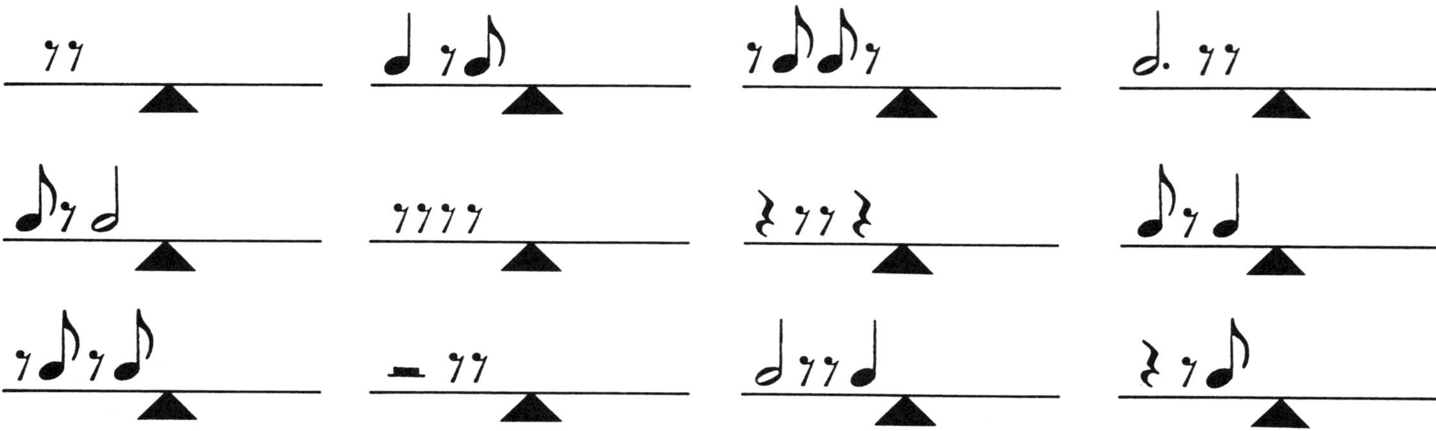

23. MUSICAL MATH

Fill in each blank square with one note or rest to solve each musical problem.

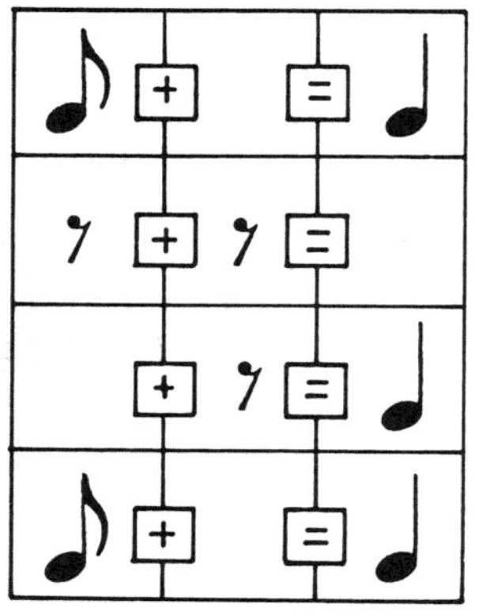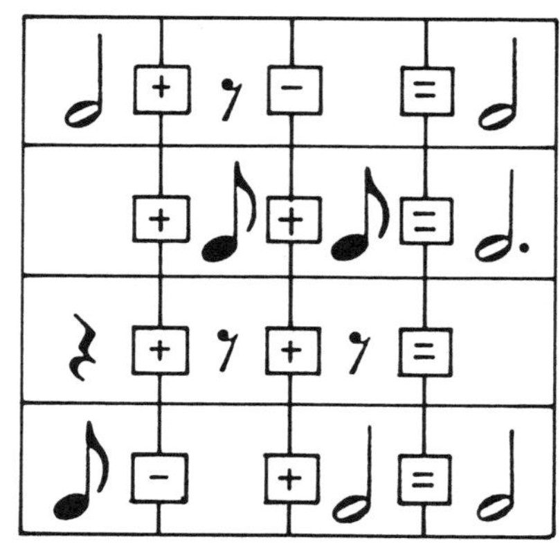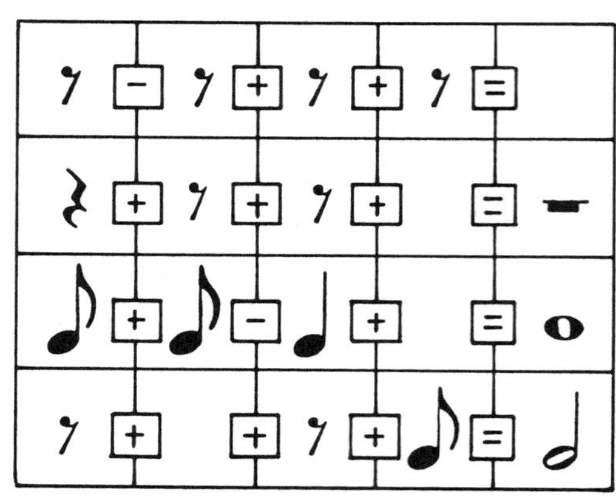

24. NAME NOTES/IDENTIFY INTERVALS

Write the name of each note on the blank provided. Write the size of each interval in the box.

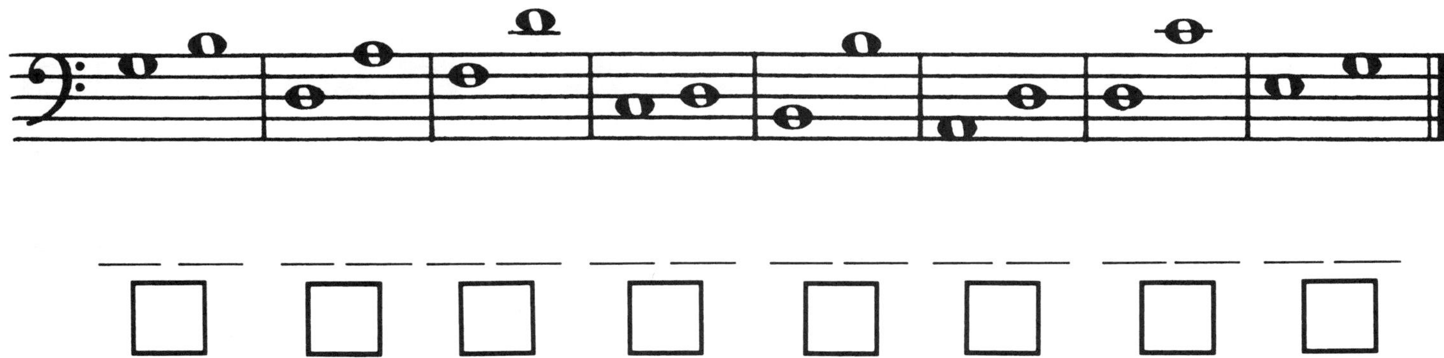

25. MUSICAL CROSSWORD PUZZLE

ACROSS

1. cancels a sharp or flat
4. distance between two notes
6. used to tune the instrument
8. a whole note = _____ quarter notes
9. the end
11. playing louds and softs
13. gradually play louder
14. play with the bow
15. play the previous music again
18. music for one instrument
21. a quarter rest = _____ count in 2/4 time
22. quick and lively
23. music for two instruments
25. eight notes apart
26. study to develop bowing and/or fingering technic

DOWN

2. short melodic passage
3. receives one beat in 4/4 time
5. the speed of music
6. play softly
7. continue in the same manner
9. the names of the spaces in the treble clef
10. musical silence
11. play each note using separate bows
12. raises a note 1/2 step
13. a person who writes music
16. moderately slow
17. the quality of a musical sound
19. connects two or more notes of different pitch
20. play loudly
24. four eighth notes = _____ quarter notes

(Answer Key—See Inside Back Cover)

26. DRAW BAR LINES/WRITE COUNTING

Draw bar lines for the three lines of music below so that each measure contains the correct number of beats. Write the counting on the blanks provided.

27. BALANCE THE SCALE

Write ONE note or rest to balance each scale.

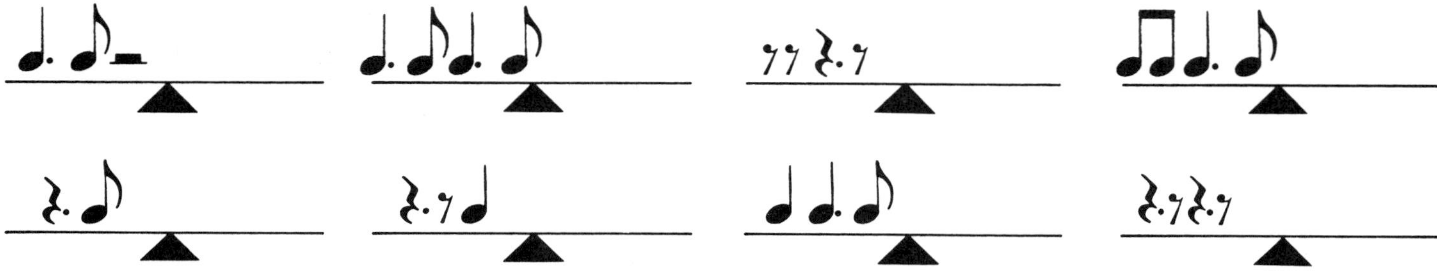

28. MUSICAL MATH

Fill in each blank square with one note or rest to solve each musical problem.

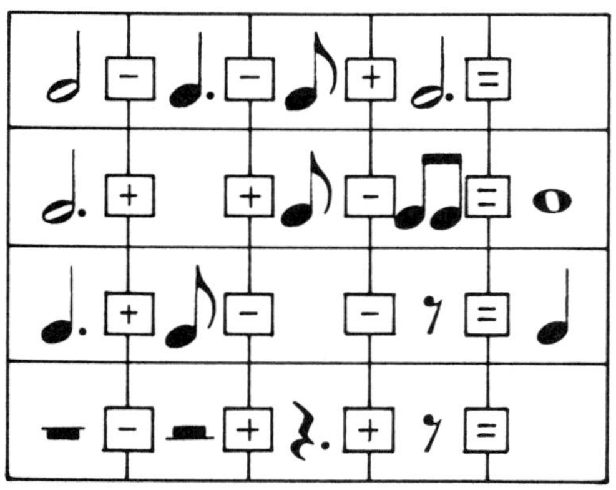 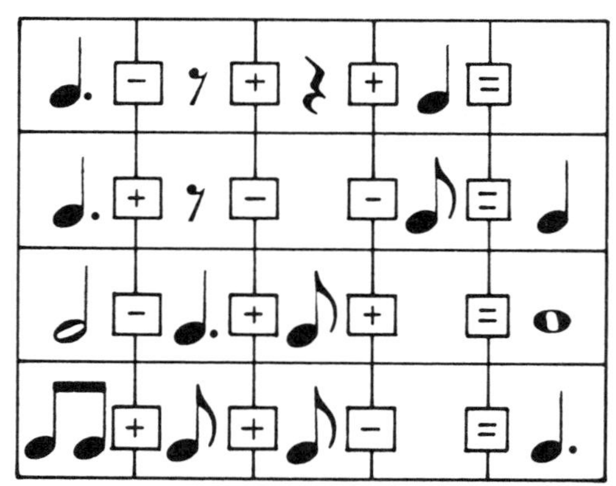

29. MUSICAL MATH

Solve each musical math problem by placing the number of the correct answer above each division line.

30. COMPLETE THE MEASURE

Complete each measure by drawing one or more of the following notes and/or rests:

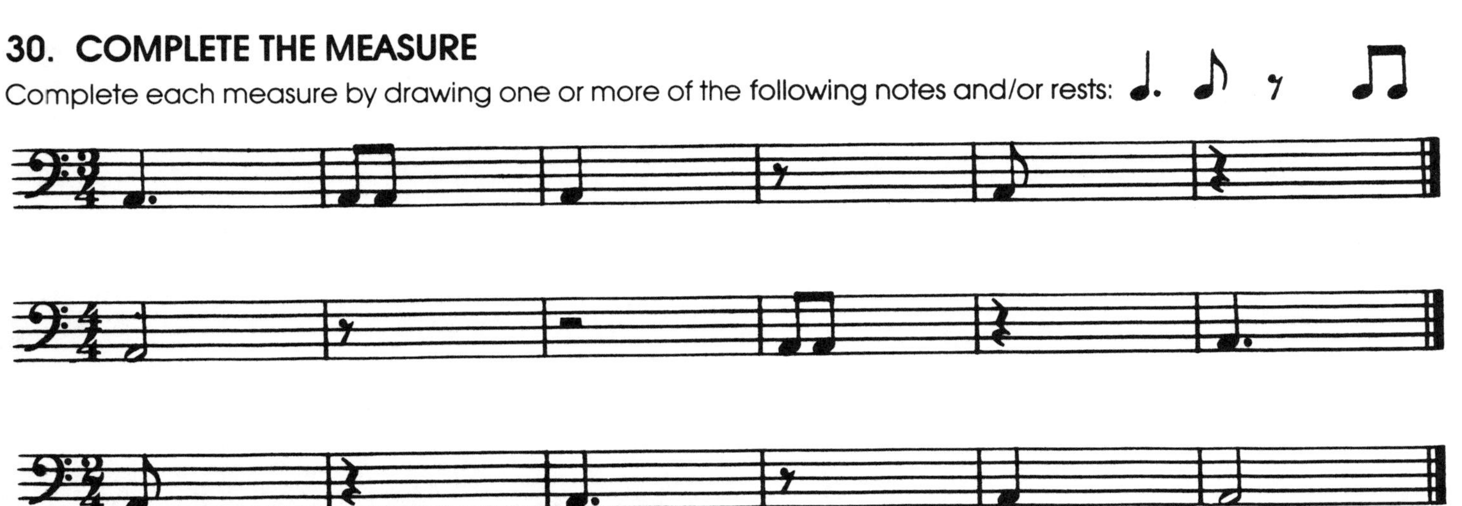

31. DRAW MUSICAL SYMBOLS

Draw the following musical symbols in the boxes.

1. flat sign
2. eighth note
3. crescendo mark
4. staccato quarter note
5. eighth rest
6. dotted quarter note
7. accented half note
8. double stop
9. diminuendo mark
10. left hand pizz.

1	2	3	4	5
6	7	8	9	10

32. FINGERING CHART

Write the name of the note that is played at the place of each circle and square on the fingering chart below.

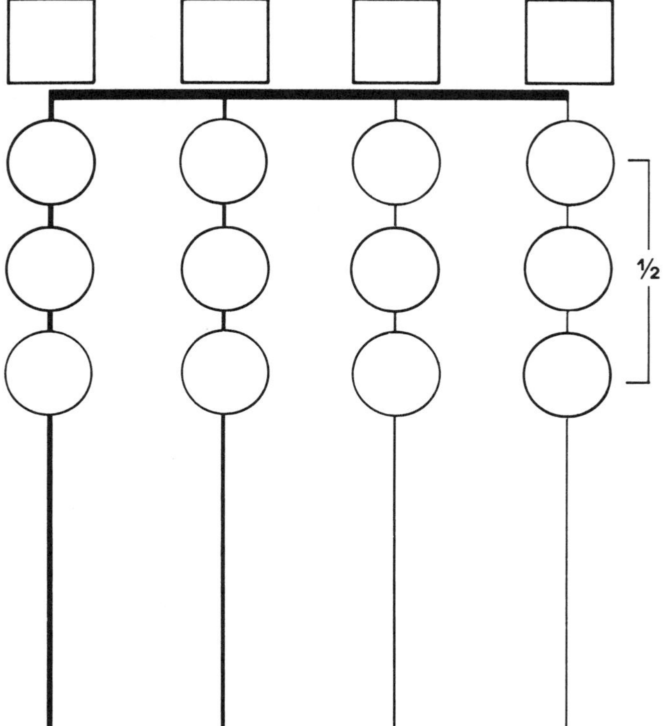

Questions:

G to A♭ is a _________________ step.

A♭ to B♭ is a _________________ step.

D to E♭ is a _________________ step.

F to G is a _________________ step.

A to B♭ is a _________________ step.

C to D is a _________________ step.

E to F is a _________________ step.

G to A is a _________________ step.

33. NAME NOTES/DRAW NOTES

① Write the name of each note on the blank provided. ② Draw the notes from the fingering chart above on the staff as requested. Use half notes. Be sure each stem points in the correct direction.

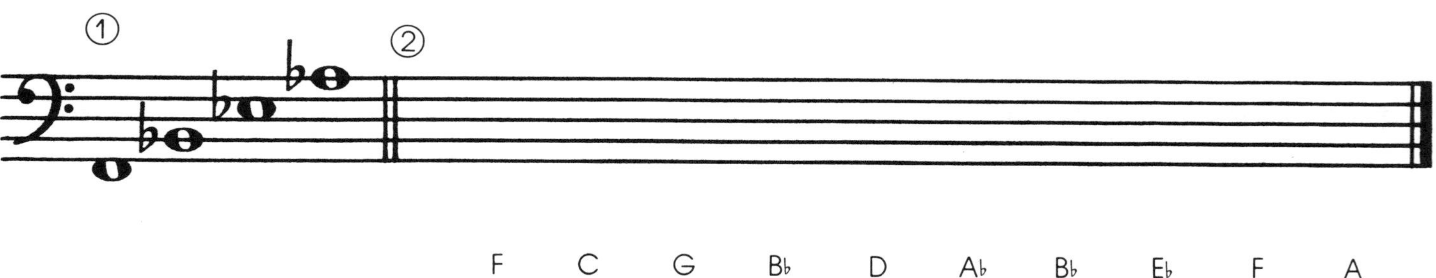

34. KEYBOARD STUDY

Write the letters on the keys for all the notes shown in the fingering chart above. Show proper relationship to middle C.

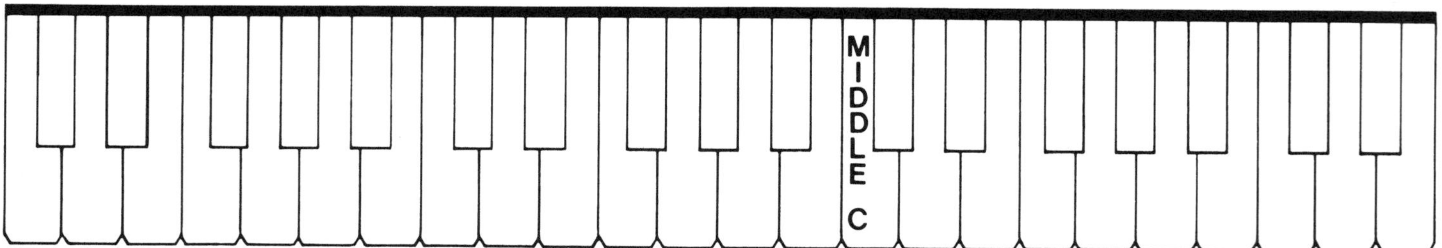

35. LEARN ENHARMONICS

Enharmonics are notes that sound the same but are written or spelled differently. Therefore, B♭ is the enharmonic of A♯. Also, E♯ is the enharmonic of F. See the keyboard below:

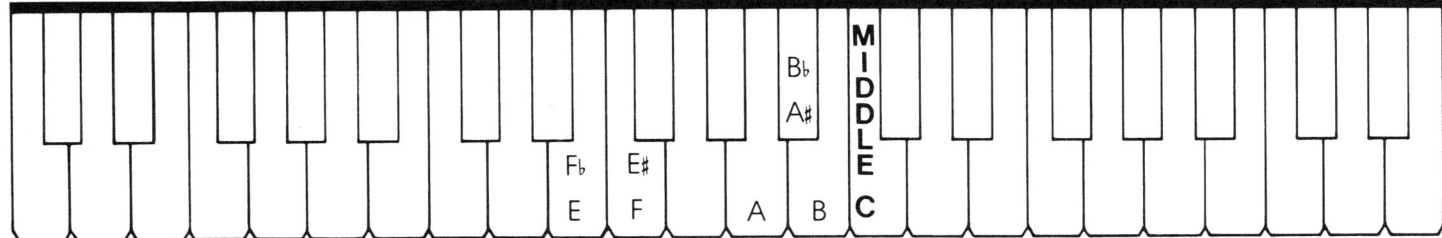

36. FIND ENHARMONICS

Write the name of each enharmonic as requested. Use the keyboard above to help determine each enharmonic.

The enharmonic of B♭ is _______________.

The enharmonic of A♭ is _______________.

The enharmonic of G♭ is _______________.

The enharmonic of E♭ is _______________.

The enharmonic of E is _______________.

The enharmonic of C is _______________.

The enharmonic of C♭ is _______________.

The enharmonic of F♭ is _______________.

The enharmonic of A♯ is _______________.

The enharmonic of D♯ is _______________.

The enharmonic of C♯ is _______________.

The enharmonic of G♯ is _______________.

The enharmonic of F is _______________.

The enharmonic of B is _______________.

The enharmonic of B♯ is _______________.

The enharmonic of E♯ is _______________.

37. IDENTIFY DYNAMICS

Draw a line to connect each word with its correct meaning and from the correct meaning to its correct symbol.

forte	soft	*mf*
mezzo forte	loud	*p*
piano	medium loud	*f*

38. NAME NOTES

1. Write the name of the note that is played at the place of each circle and square on the fingering chart. These notes form the F arpeggio.
2. The notes on the staff below are in the F arpeggio. Write the name of each note on the blank provided.

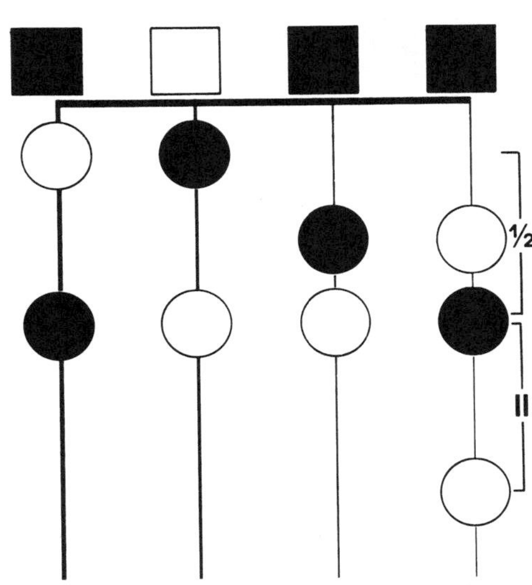

39. DRAW HALF STEPS

① Draw a quarter note that is a half step ABOVE the given note. Use the example as a model. Refer to the keyboard below if necessary.
② Draw a half note that is a half step BELOW the given note. Use the example as a model.

KEYBOARD

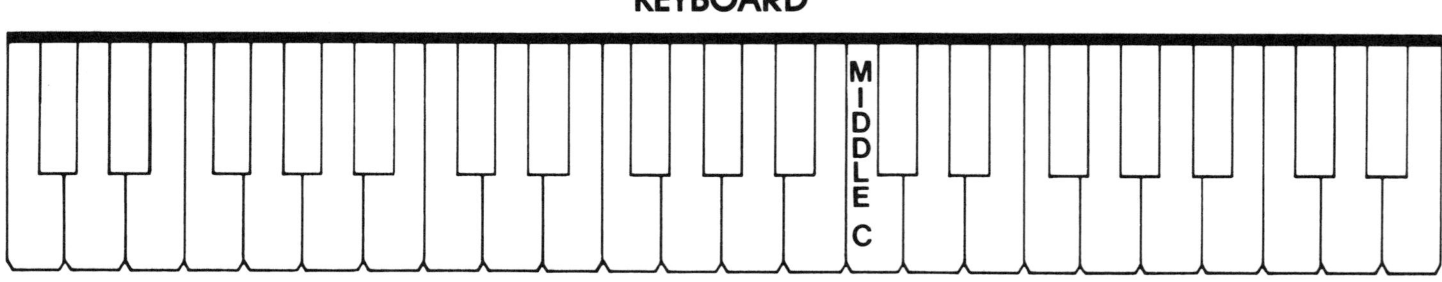

40. DRAW WHOLE STEPS

① Draw a half note that is a whole step ABOVE the given note. Use the example as a model. Refer to the keyboard above if necessary.
② Draw a quarter note that is a whole step BELOW the given note. Use the example as a model.

41. MUSICAL MATH

Solve each musical math problem by placing the number of the correct answer above each division line.

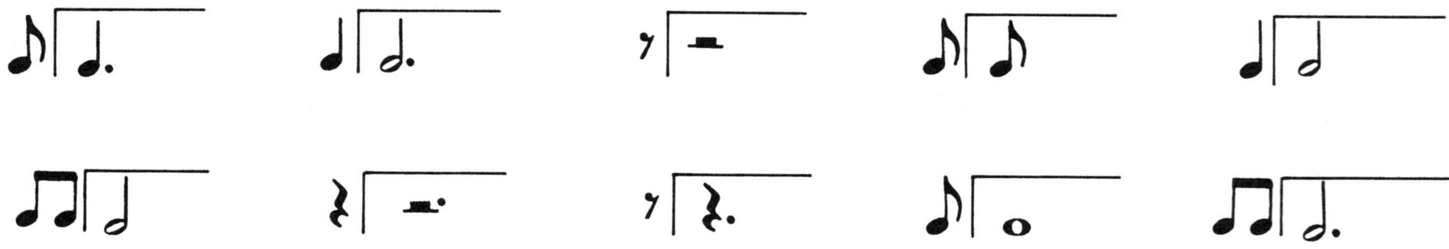

42. LEARN ABOUT MINOR SCALES

For every major scale there is a relative (related) minor scale with the same key signature. The relative minor scale begins on the 6th note of the major scale and ascends for 8 notes. e.g. d minor is the relative minor to F Major.

There are three types of minor scales. Each scale has the whole steps and half steps arranged in a slightly different order. See the chart below. Each minor scale begins with a minor tetrachord. The second tetrachord undergoes changes in the placement of the 1/2 step by the use of accidentals.

43. DRAW MAJOR AND MINOR TETRACHORDS

1. Draw the notes of the Major and minor tetrachords as indicated. Use whole notes.
2. Name the notes of each tetrachord on the blank provided.

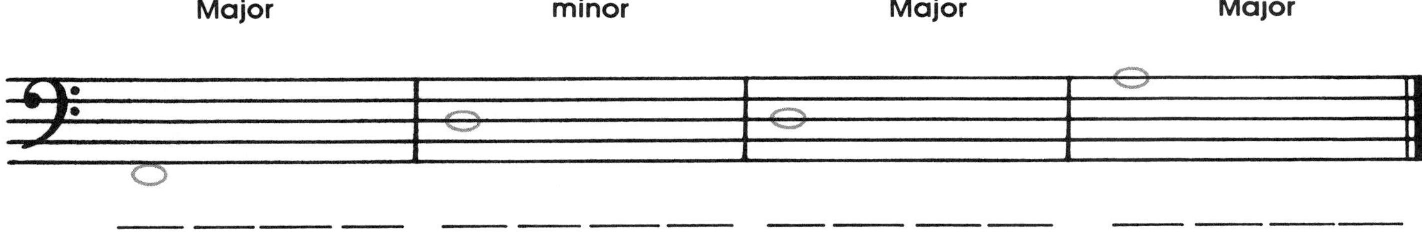

44. DRAW MINOR SCALES

1. Draw the notes of the three d minor scales on the staff as requested. Use half notes.
2. Write the name of each note on the blank provided.

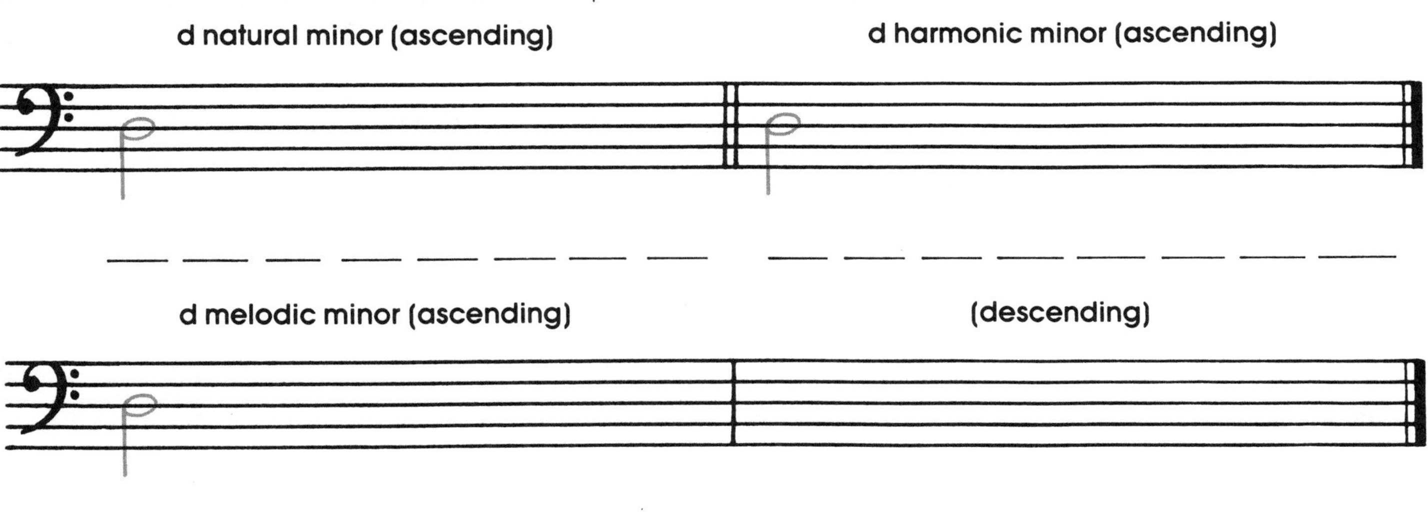

45. IDENTIFY HIGH AND LOW NOTES

Identify the fingering for each of the notes in ½ position as follows: On the blanks provided, place a **1** for notes played with the first finger and a **2** for notes played with the second finger.

46. NAME NOTES

1. Write the name of the note that is played at the place of each circle and square on the fingering chart. These notes form the B♭ arpeggio.
2. The notes on the staff below are in the B♭ arpeggio. Write the name of each note on the blank provided.

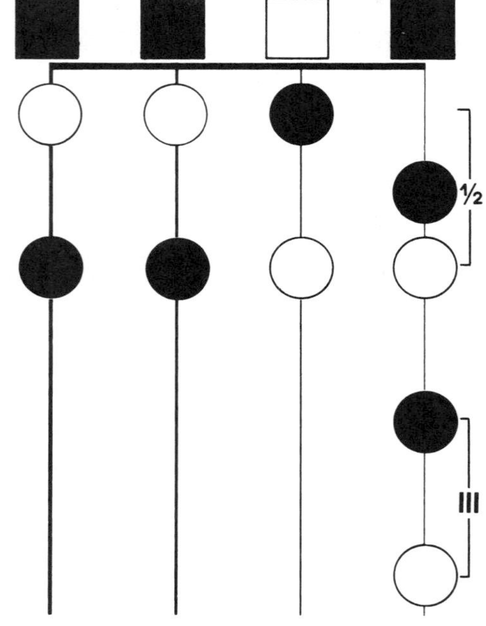

47. IDENTIFY HIGH AND LOW NOTES

Identify the fingering for each of the notes in 1st position as follows: On the blanks provided, place a **4** for notes played with the fourth finger and a **2** for notes played with the second finger.

48. NAME AND DRAW ARPEGGIOS

Name the notes in the C, F and B♭ arpeggios on the blanks provided. Draw all the notes of the C, F and B♭ arpeggios that you have learned. Use quarter notes. Be sure each stem points in the correct direction.

C   F   B♭

49. DRAW MAJOR AND MINOR TETRACHORDS

1. Draw the notes of the Major and minor tetrachords as indicated. Use whole notes.
2. Name the notes of each tetrachord on the blank provided.

Major   **minor**   **Major**   **Major**

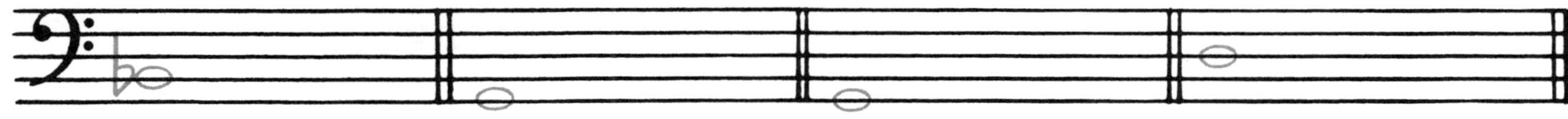

50. DRAW A MELODIC MINOR SCALE

1. Draw the notes of the g melodic minor scale on the staff below. Use quarter notes. Be sure each stem points in the correct direction.
2. Write the name of each note on the blank provided.

g melodic minor (ascending)   **(descending)**

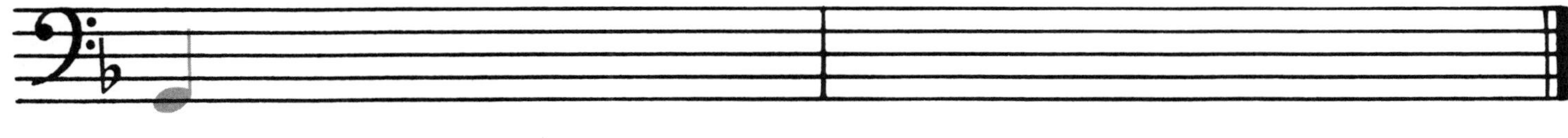

51. MUSICAL MATH

Fill in each blank with the number that solves each musical problem.

52. COMPOSE MUSIC

Draw your clef, a key signature and a time signature. Write phrases in a minor key using the notes, rhythms and rests you have learned.

53. DRAW BAR LINES/WRITE COUNTING

Draw bar lines for the two lines of music below so that each measure contains the correct number of beats. Write the counting on the blanks provided.

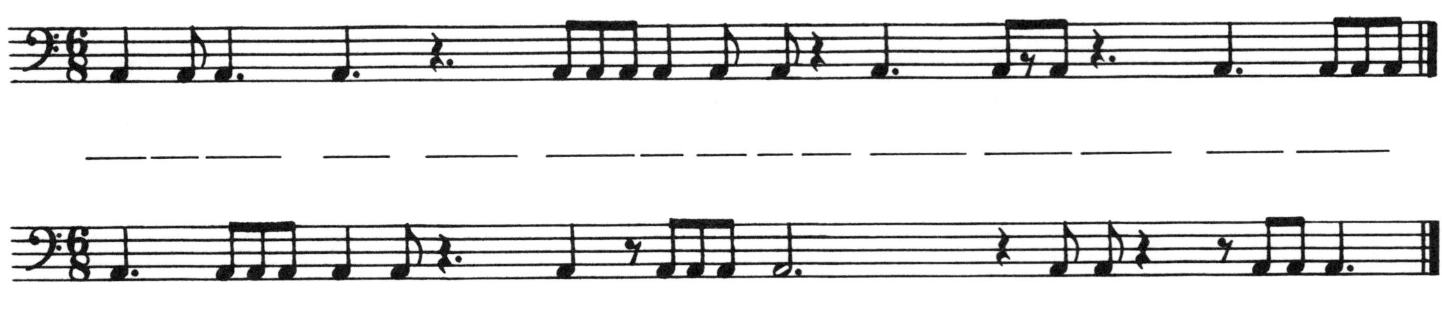

54. BALANCE THE SCALE IN 6/8 TIME

Write ONE note or rest to balance each scale.

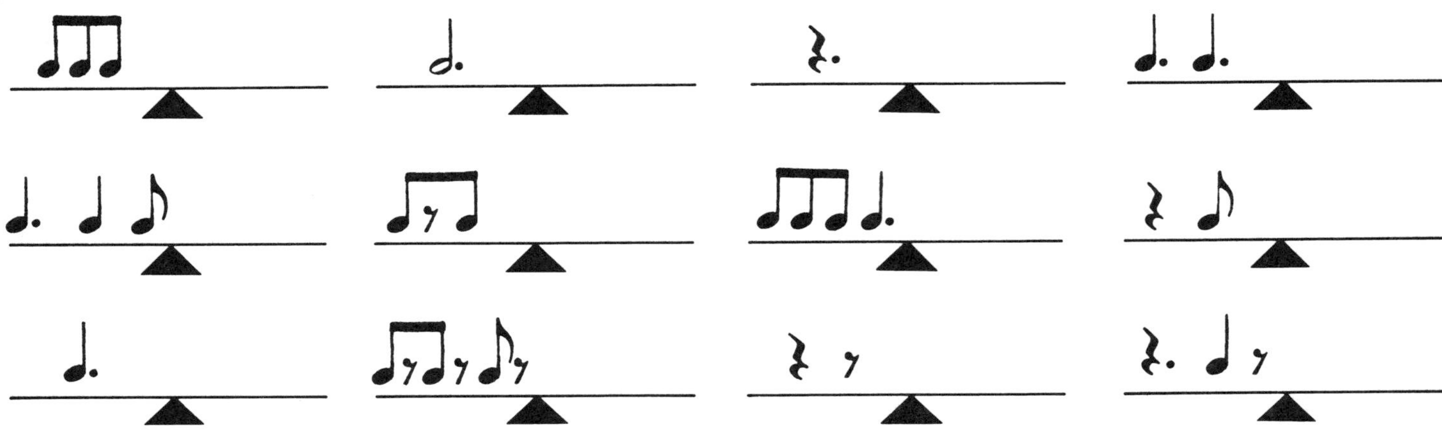

55. DRAW KEY SIGNATURES

Draw the key signatures on the staff as requested. Place the tonic note (key tone) on the staff. Use whole notes.

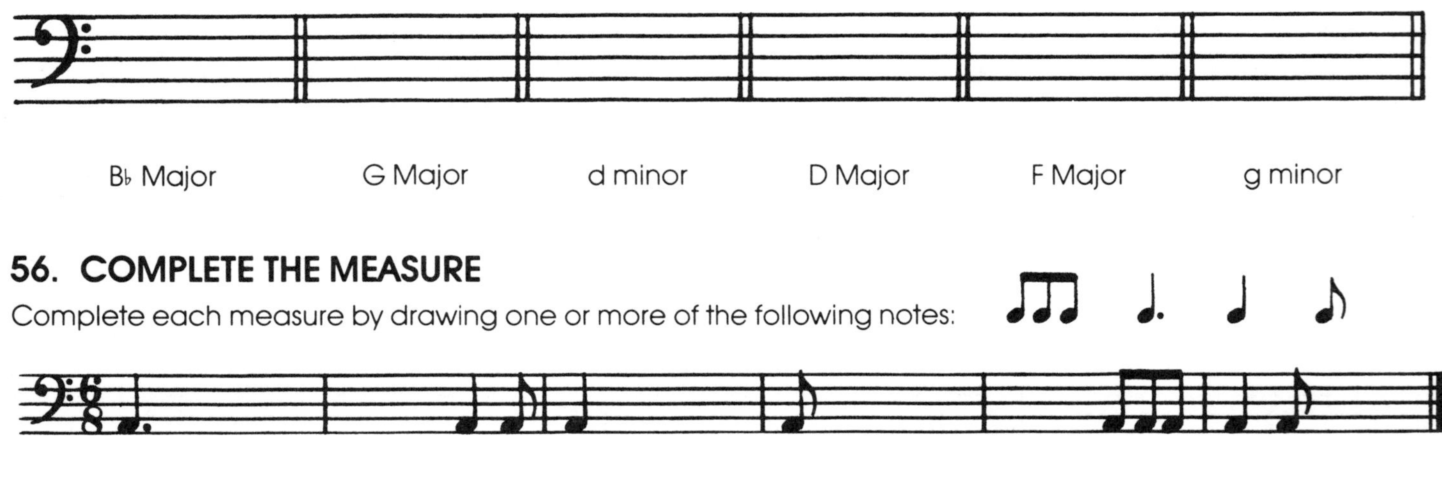

56. COMPLETE THE MEASURE

Complete each measure by drawing one or more of the following notes:

57. IDENTIFY MAJOR AND MINOR SCALES

Write the letter name and scale name on the blanks provided, e.g. e minor. Mark ½ steps.

58. WORD SEARCH

24 musical words are hidden in the puzzle below. Can you find them? Be sure to look horizontally, vertically and diagonally and then circle each word that you find. A list of words is found on each side of the puzzle.

Q	R	Y	K	E	Y	B	O	A	R	D	L	X	S
H	S	Z	T	E	G	M	M	C	O	M	O	X	B
W	R	A	V	N	T	D	G	D	O	D	U	Y	P
R	L	T	I	E	N	U	R	G	S	O	R	J	Z
F	H	N	E	U	I	T	D	N	J	U	E	I	Q
M	U	Y	O	C	E	G	E	E	X	B	Z	J	I
T	A	R	T	L	H	L	H	M	E	L	O	D	Y
K	E	J	P	H	B	N	H	T	M	E	D	P	L
V	E	I	O	M	M	F	I	F	H	S	U	T	J
M	R	Y	E	R	W	E	J	C	R	T	E	R	Q
T	I	S	F	E	R	M	A	T	A	O	T	I	U
S	N	N	T	D	I	V	I	S	I	P	G	O	N
E	E	O	O	A	E	P	I	C	K	U	P	B	C
W	S	H	A	R	P	X	P	R	I	T	A	R	D

Word list (left): DIVISI, DOUBLESTOP, DUET, EIGHTH, ENSEMBLE, ETUDE, FERMATA, FLAT, FROG, KEY, KEYBOARD, LOURE

Word list (right): MAJOR, MELODY, MINOR, PICKUP, RHYTHM, RITARD, ROUND, SHARP, TECHNIC, TRIO, TRIPLET, TUNING

(Answer Key—
See Inside Back Cover)

59. MUSICAL MATH

Fill in the left blank square with one note or rest to equal the correct total value. Fill in the right blank square with the correct total value.

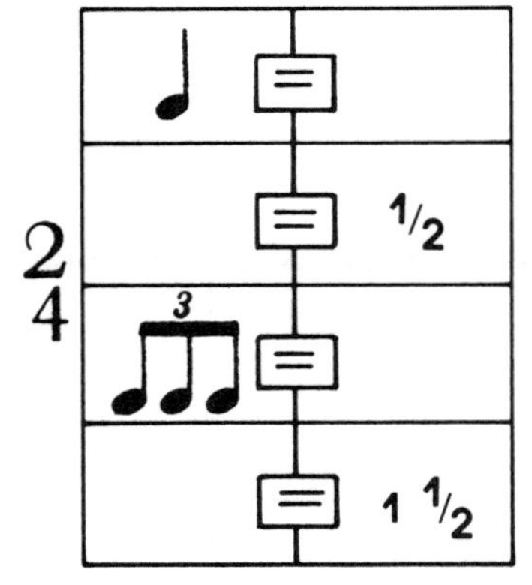

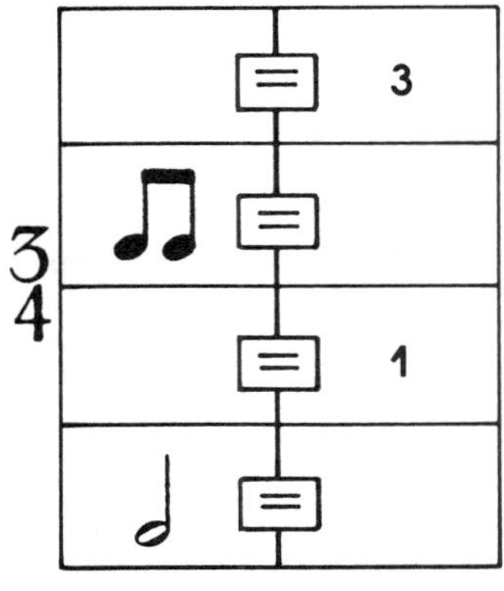

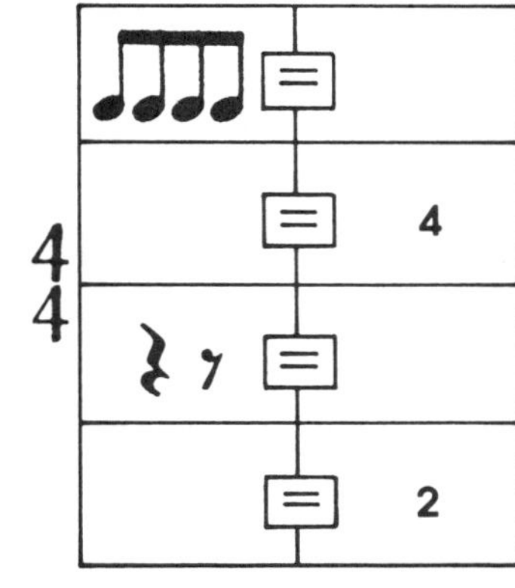

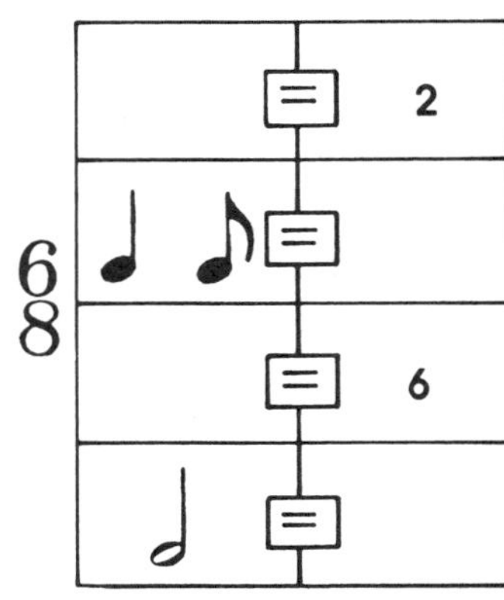

60. FINGERING CHART

Write the name of the note that is played at the place of each circle and square on the fingering chart below.

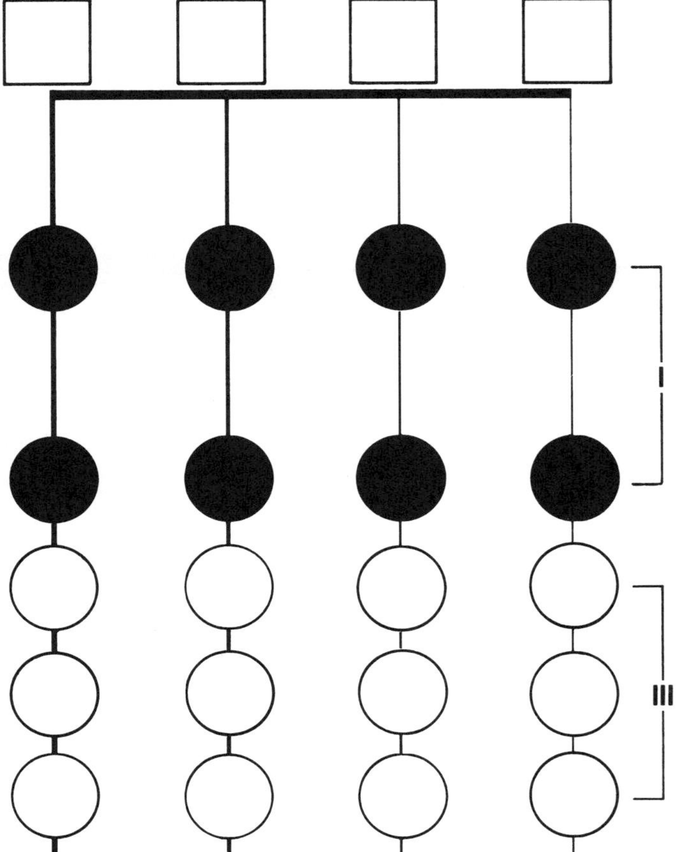

Questions:

G to A is a _________________ step.

C♯ to D is a _________________ step.

D to E is a _________________ step.

G♯ to A is a _________________ step.

C to D is a _________________ step.

D♯ to E is a _________________ step.

C to D is a _________________ step.

G♯ to A♯ is a _________________ step.

61. NAME NOTES/DRAW NOTES

① Write the name of each note on the blank provided. ② Draw the notes from the fingering chart above on the staff as indicated. Use quarter and half notes. Be sure each stem points in the correct direction.

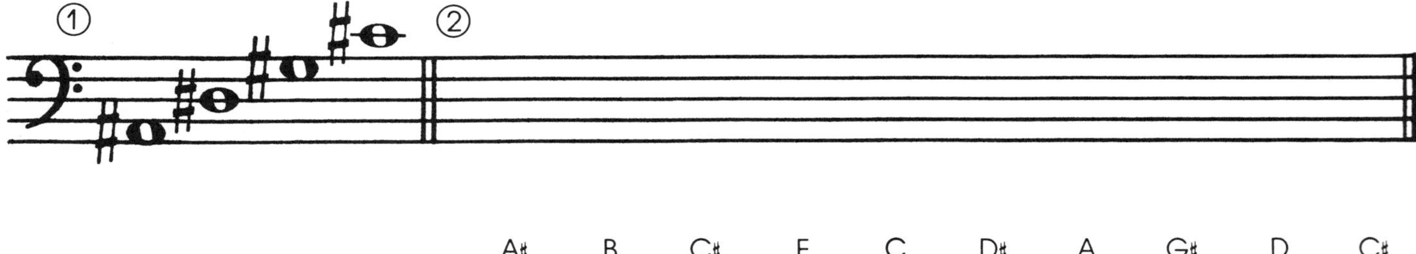

62. KEYBOARD STUDY

Write the letters on the keys for all the notes in the fingering chart above. Show proper relationship to middle C.

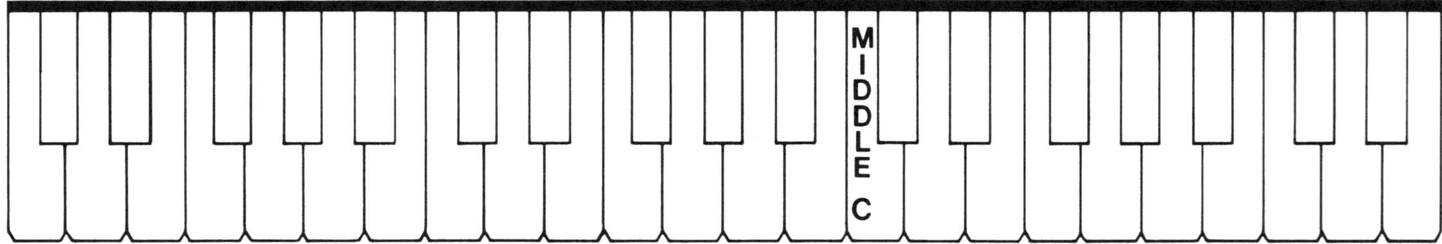

63. NAME NOTES

1. Write the name of each note that is played at the place of each circle and square on the fingering chart. These notes form the A arpeggio.
2. The notes on the staff below are in the A arpeggio. Write the name of each note on the blank provided.

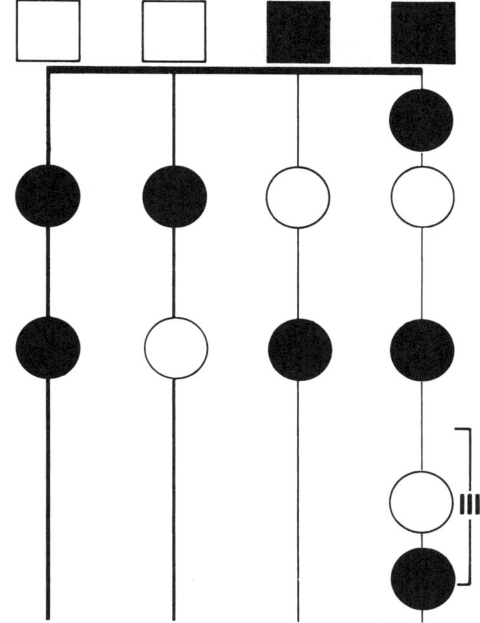

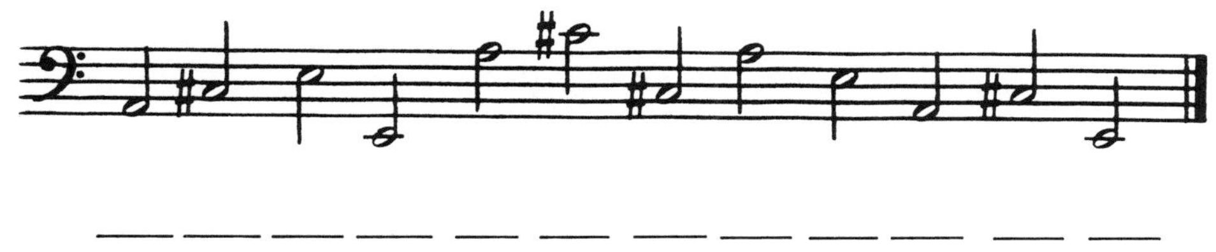

64. IDENTIFY HIGH AND LOW NOTES

Identify the fingering for each note in ½ position as follows: On the blanks provided, place a **1** for notes played with the first finger and a **2** for notes played with a second finger.

65. DRAW MAJOR AND MINOR TETRACHORDS

1. Draw the notes of the Major and minor tetrachords as indicated. Use whole notes.
2. Name the notes of each tetrachord on the blank provided.

Major   Major   Major   minor

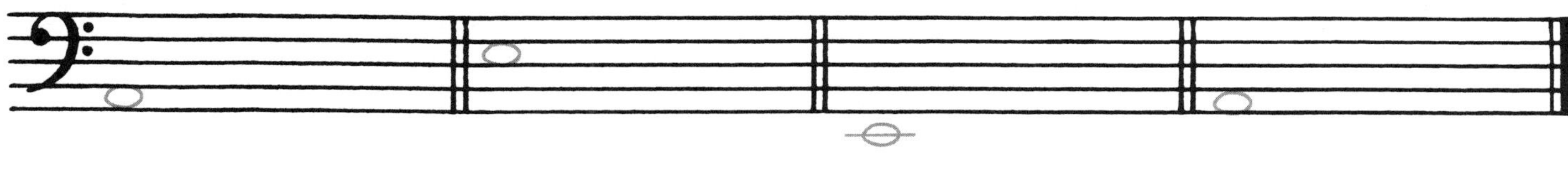

66. IDENTIFY WHOLE AND HALF STEPS

Write the size of each interval in the box provided. e.g. whole step ⬚1 half step ⬚½

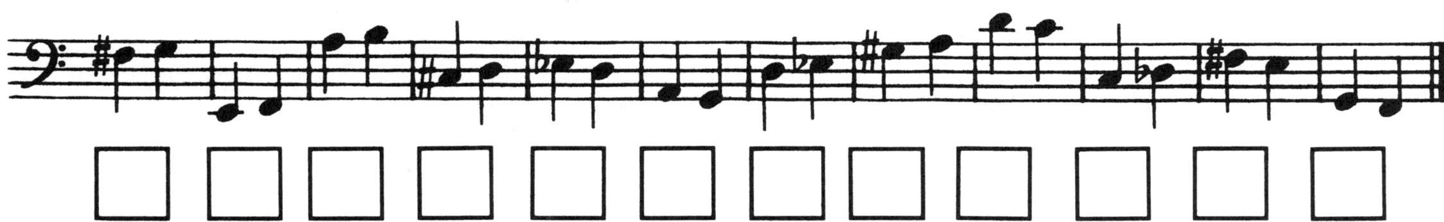

67. DRAW AND NAME ENHARMONIC NOTES

Write the name of each enharmonic note on the blank provided. Draw both notes on the staff with the accidental to the left of the notehead. Use quarter notes. Be sure each stem points in the correct direction.

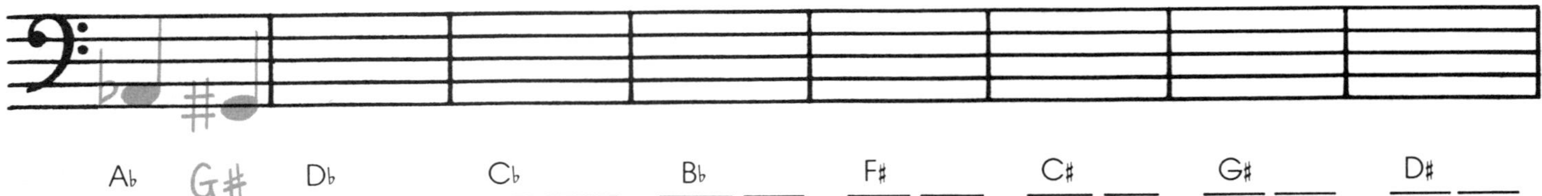

68. DRAW A CHROMATIC SCALE

Draw the notes of an ascending G chromatic scale. Name the notes on the blanks provided. Use half notes. Be sure each stem points in the correct direction.

69. DRAW BAR LINES/WRITE COUNTING

Draw bar lines for the two lines of music below so that each measure contains the correct number of beats. Write the counting on the blanks provided.

70. BALANCE THE SCALE

Write ONE note or rest to balance each scale.

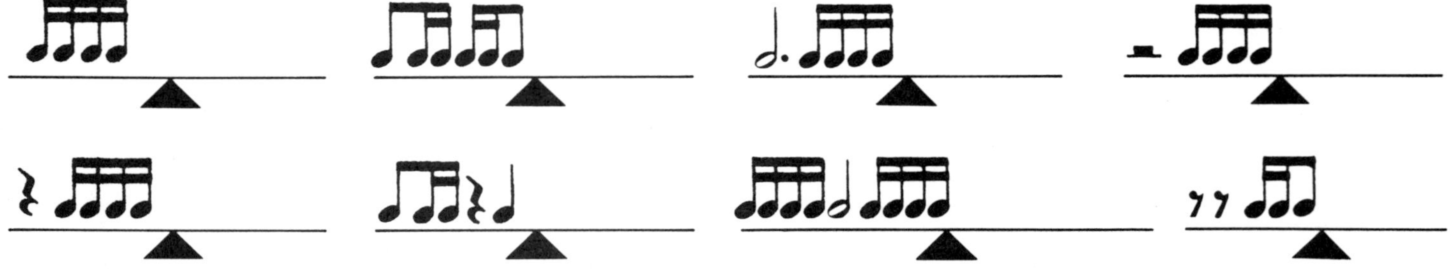

71. COMPLETE THE MEASURE

Complete each measure by drawing one or more of the following notes and/or rests: 

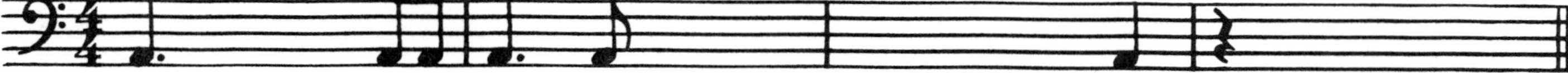

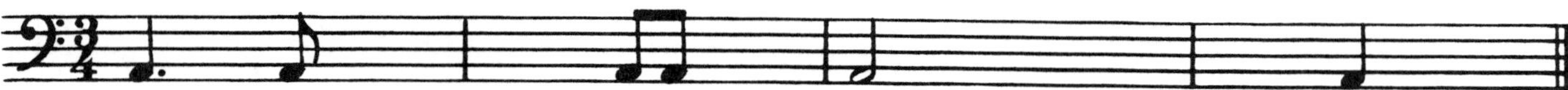

72. DRAW BAR LINES/WRITE COUNTING

Draw bar lines for the two lines of music below so that each measure contains the correct number of beats. Write the counting on the blanks provided.

73. COMPOSE MUSIC

Write a composition to play for your class. Draw your clef, a key signature and a time signature. Write 4 measure phrases in AABA or Theme and Variation form using the notes and rhythms you have learned. Add the appropriate tempo marking, dynamices, and bowings needed. Make up a title for your composition.

____
(Title)

74. MATCHING

Place the letter of the correct answer in the space opposite the definition.

GENERAL KNOWLEDGE

_______ 1. conditions the bow for playing

_______ 2. music for one instrument

_______ 3. music for several players together

_______ 4. playing two strings together

_______ 5. playing with the bow

_______ 6. distance between two notes

PLAYING POSITIONS

_______ 7. necessary for a good right hand position

_______ 8. necessary for good finger placement

_______ 9. in a straight line with the bridge

_______ 10. direction the bow stick leans

_______ 11. necessary for a good left hand position

_______ 12. proper placement of left thumb

_______ 13. exercise to strengthen right hand

_______ 14. necessary for good tone quality

TUNING

_______ 15. proper attachment of a metal string

_______ 16. proper attachment of a gut wound string (except string bass)

_______ 17. common reference pitch

_______ 18. distance between open strings

_______ 19. to lower the pitch

_______ 20. to raise the pitch

VIBRATO

_______ 21. keywords to developing vibrato

_______ 22. correct vibrato motion

a. bow pressed into the string

b. thumb bent

c. double stops

d. to a string adjuster

e. toward the fingerboard

f. fingernails cut short

g. bow stroke

h. turn the peg backward

i. to the tail piece

j. wrist straight

k. four (4) notes

l. piano

m. solo

n. interval

o. ensemble

p. rosin

q. strong and relaxed

r. arco

s. squeeze-relax

t. slow and relaxed

u. behind 2nd finger

v. turn the peg forward

75. IDENTIFY MUSICAL SIGNS

Identify each abbreviation or sign and tell what you are to do.

1. _______________________

2. _______________________

3. _______________________

4. _______________________

5. *mf* _______________________

6. _______________________

7. ⑤ ⑨ ⑬ _______________________

8. _______________________

9. _______________________

10. _______________________

11. W.B. _______________________

12. _______________________

13. _______________________

14. _______________________

15. *f* _______________________

16. _______________________

17. _______________________

18. L.H. _______________________

19. _______________________

20. *p* _______________________

21. _______________________

22. U.H. _______________________

23. _______________________

24. V _______________________

25. ♭ _______________________

26. _______________________

27. _______________________

28. _______________________

29. _______________________

30. _______________________

76. FINGERING CHART

Write the name of the note that is played at the place of each circle and square on the fingering chart below. Write the correct key signature.

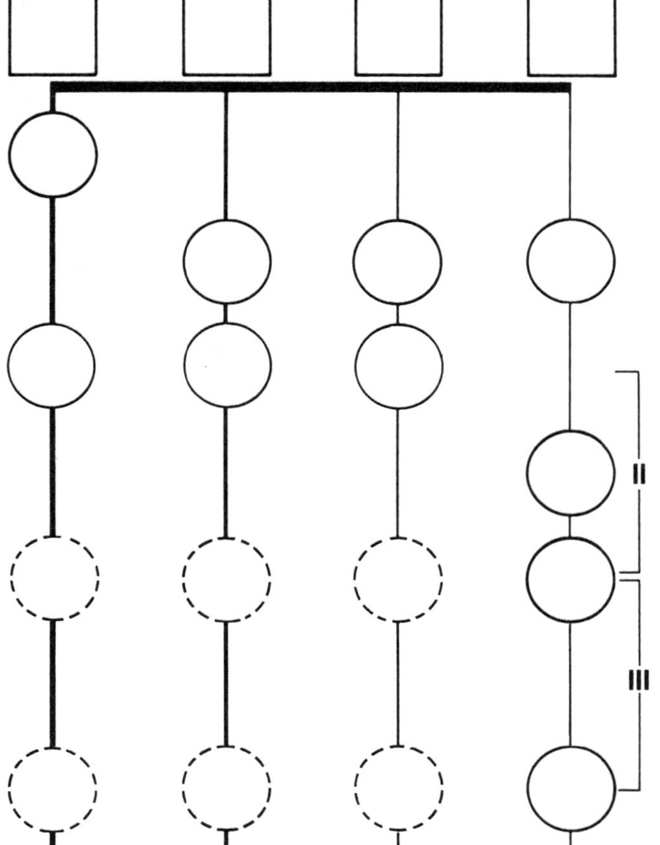

Questions:

This is the key of ________________________.

The key of _______ has _____________ sharps.

The half steps in the key of _______________

are ______ to ______ and ______ to __________.

77. DRAW NOTES/NAME NOTES

Draw a note on the staff for each note shown in the fingering chart above. (low to high) Use whole notes. Name the notes on the blanks provided, add the key signature, and place half step markings where appropriate.

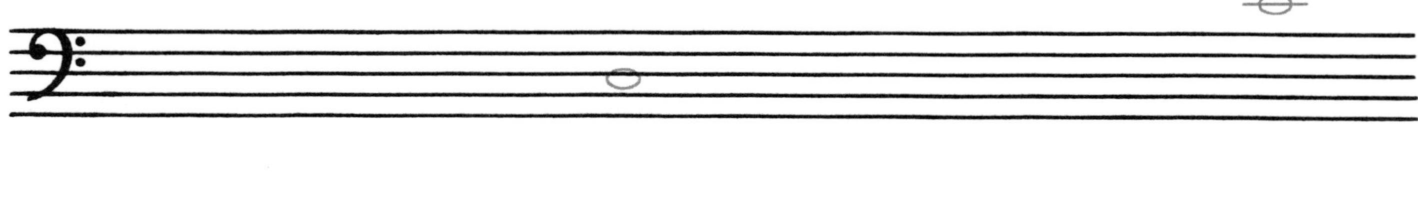

78. KEYBOARD STUDY

Write the letters on the keys for the one octave C Major scale. Show proper relationship to middle C.

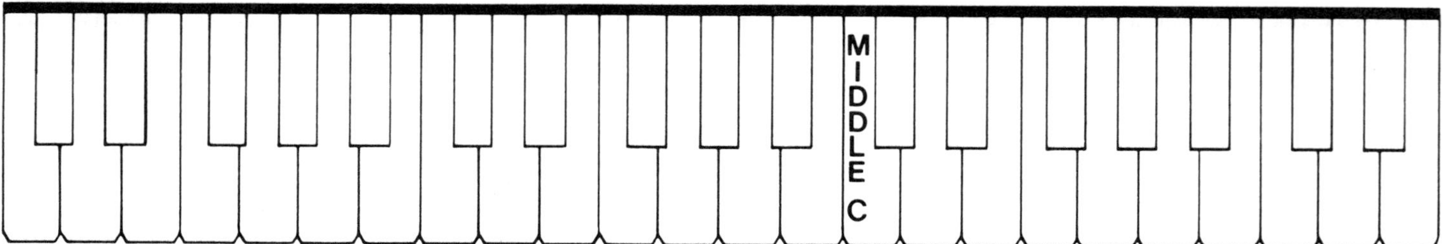

79. FINGERING CHART

Write the name of the note that is played at the place of each circle and square on the fingering chart below. Place the sharps from the diagram on the staff to form the correct key signature.

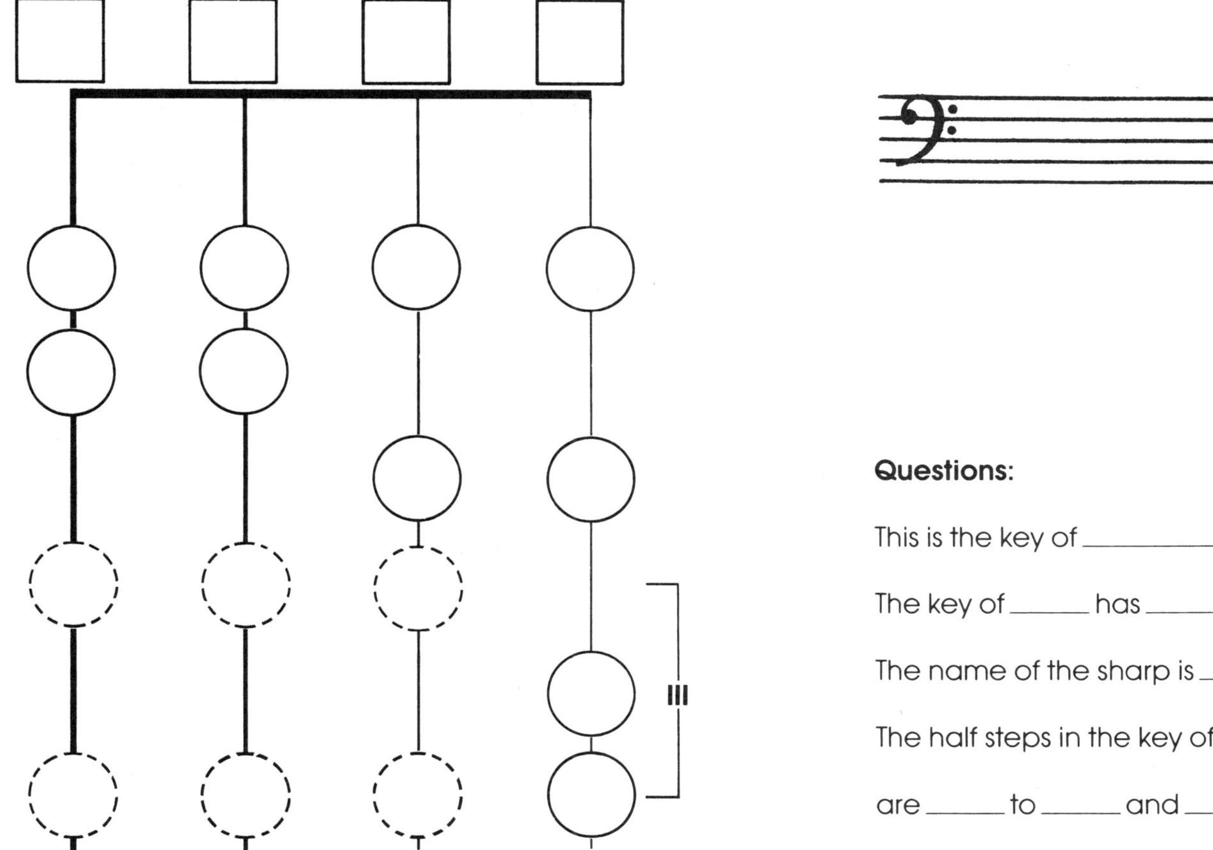

Questions:

This is the key of ________________.

The key of ______ has ____________ sharp.

The name of the sharp is ____________.

The half steps in the key of ____________

are ______ to ______ and ______ to ________.

80. DRAW NOTES/NAME NOTES

Draw a note on the staff for each note shown in the fingering chart above. (low to high) Use whole notes. Name the notes on the blanks provided, add the key signature, and place half step markings where appropriate.

81. KEYBOARD STUDY

Write the letters on the keys for the one octave G Major scale. Show proper relationship to middle C.

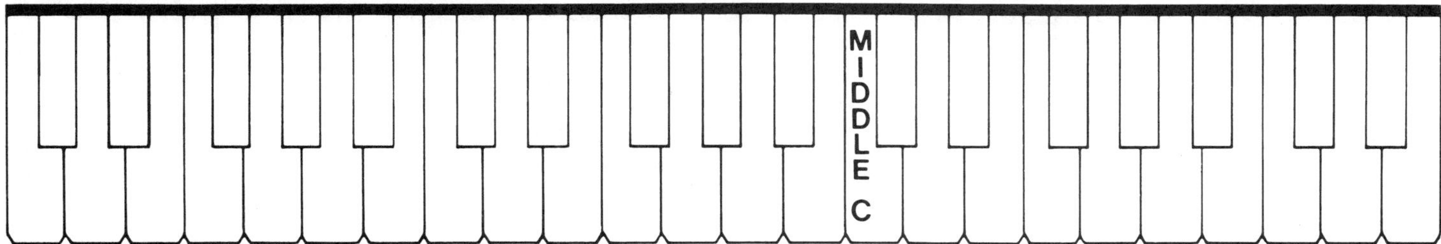

82. FINGERING CHART

Write the name of the note that is played at the place of each circle and square on the fingering chart below. Place the sharps from the diagram on the staff to form the correct key signature.

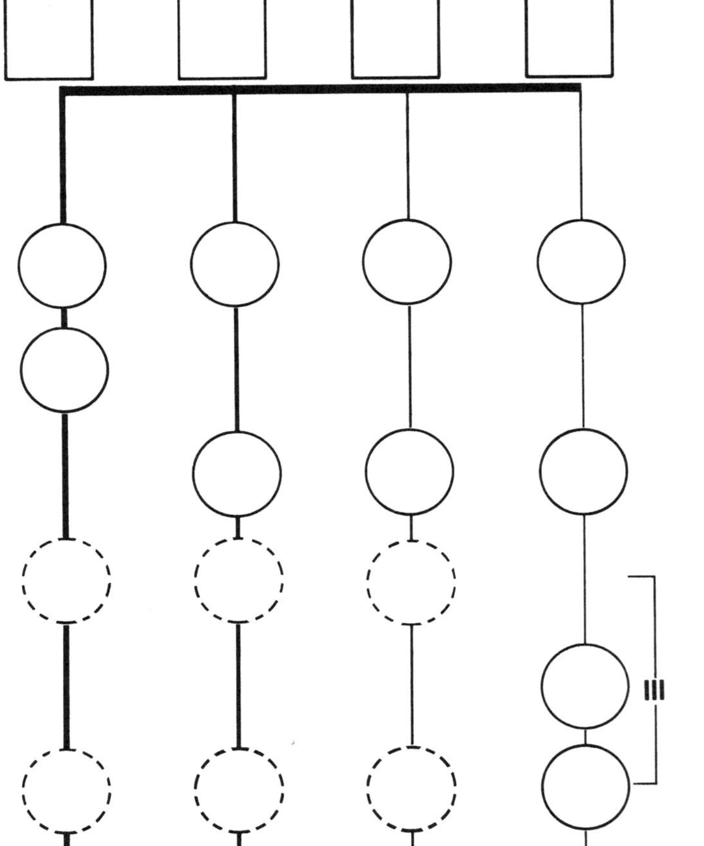

Questions:

This is the key of ________________________ .

The key of ______ has __________________ sharps.

The sharps are ______ and ________________ .

The half steps in the key of __________________

are ______ to ______ and ______ to __________ .

83. DRAW NOTES/NAME NOTES

Draw a note on the staff for each note shown in the fingering chart above. (low to high) Use whole notes. Name the notes on the blanks provided, add the key signature, and place half step markings where appropriate.

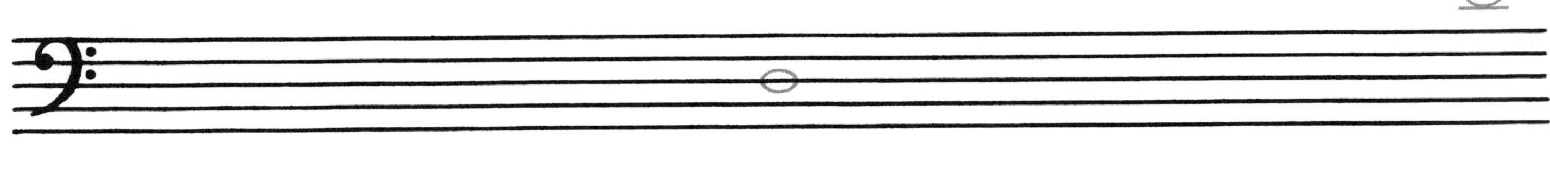

84. KEYBOARD STUDY

Write the letters on the keys for the one octave D Major scale. Show proper relationship to middle C.

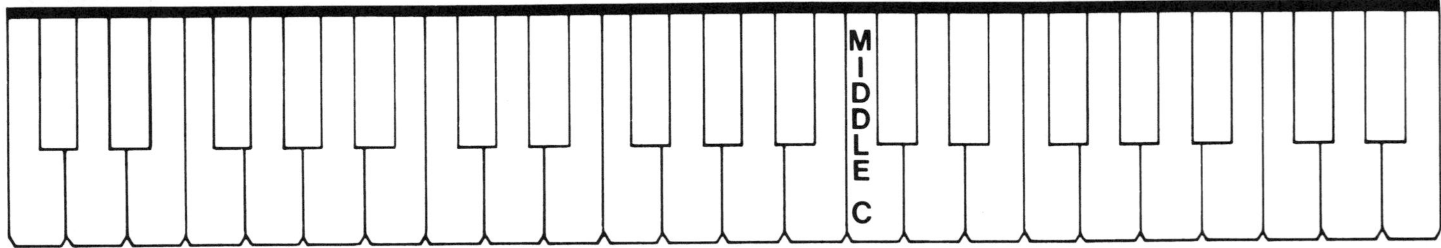

85. FINGERING CHART

Write the name of the note that is played at the place of each circle and square on the fingering chart below.
Place the sharps from the diagram on the staff to form the correct key signature.

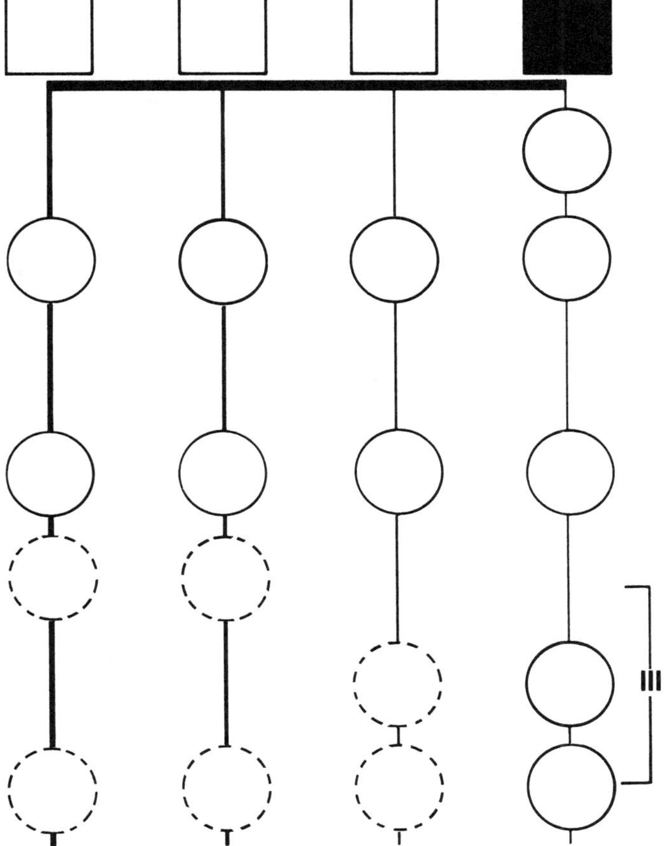

Questions:

This is the key of ___________________.

The key of _______ has _______________ sharps.

The sharps are _______, _______ and ___________.

The half steps in the key of _______________

are _______ to _______ and _______ to ___________.

86. DRAW NOTES/NAME NOTES

Draw a note on the staff for each note shown in the fingering chart above. (low to high) Use whole notes.
Name the notes on the blanks provided, add the key signature, and place half step markings where
appropriate.

87. KEYBOARD STUDY

Write the letters on the keys for the one octave A Major scale. Show proper relationship to middle C.

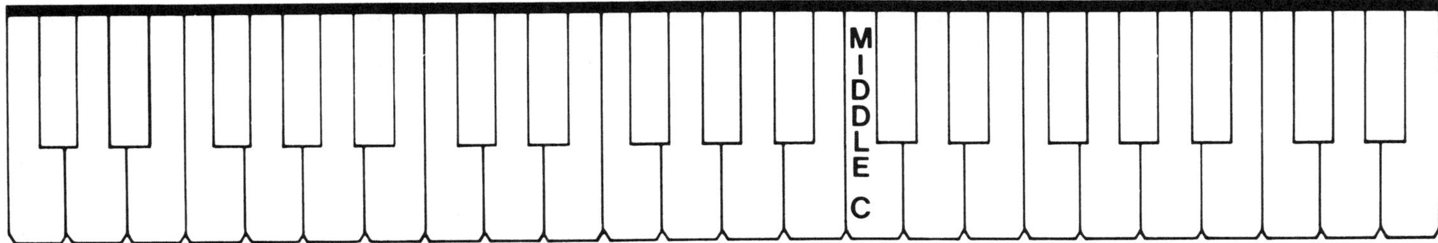

88. FINGERING CHART

Write the name of the note that is played at the place of each circle and square on the fingering chart below.
Place the flats from the diagram on the staff to form the correct key signature.

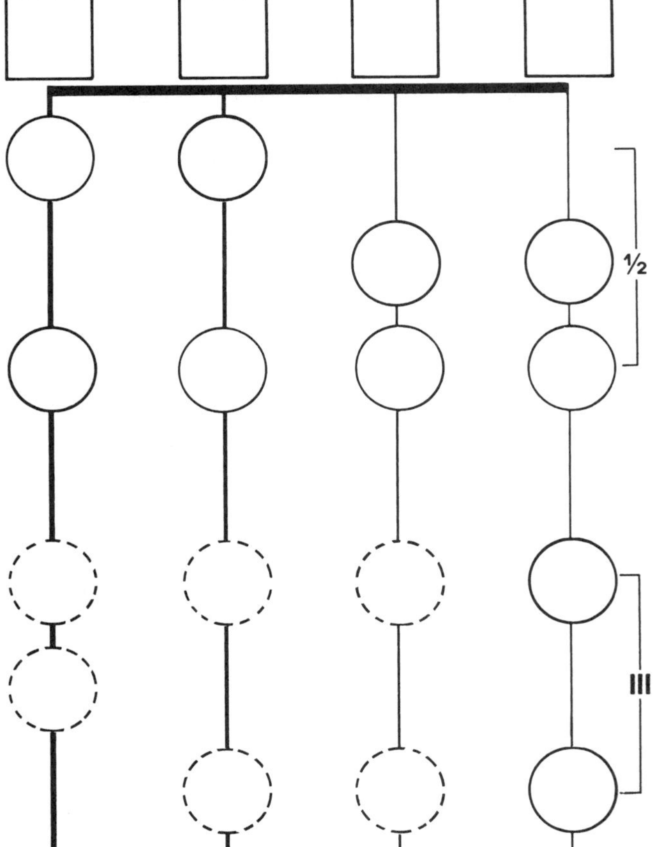

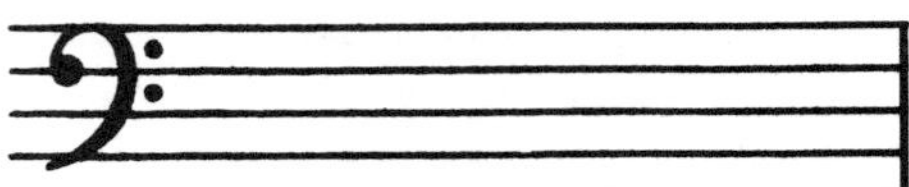

Questions:

This is the key of ________________________________ .

The key of _______ has __________________ flat.

The name of the flat is __________________ .

The half steps in the key of ____________________

are _______ to _______ and _______ to __________ .

89. DRAW NOTES/NAME NOTES

Draw a note on the staff for each note shown in the fingering chart above. (low to high) Use whole notes.
Name the notes on the blanks provided, add the key signature, and place half step markings where
appropriate.

90. KEYBOARD STUDY

Write the letters on the keys for the one octave F Major scale. Show proper relationship to middle C.

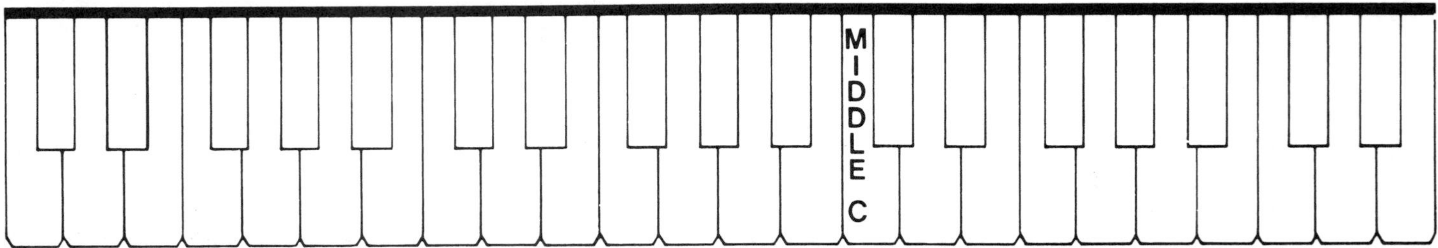

91. FINGERING CHART

Write the name of the note that is played at the place of each circle and square on the fingering chart below.
Place the flats from the diagram on the staff to form the correct key signature.

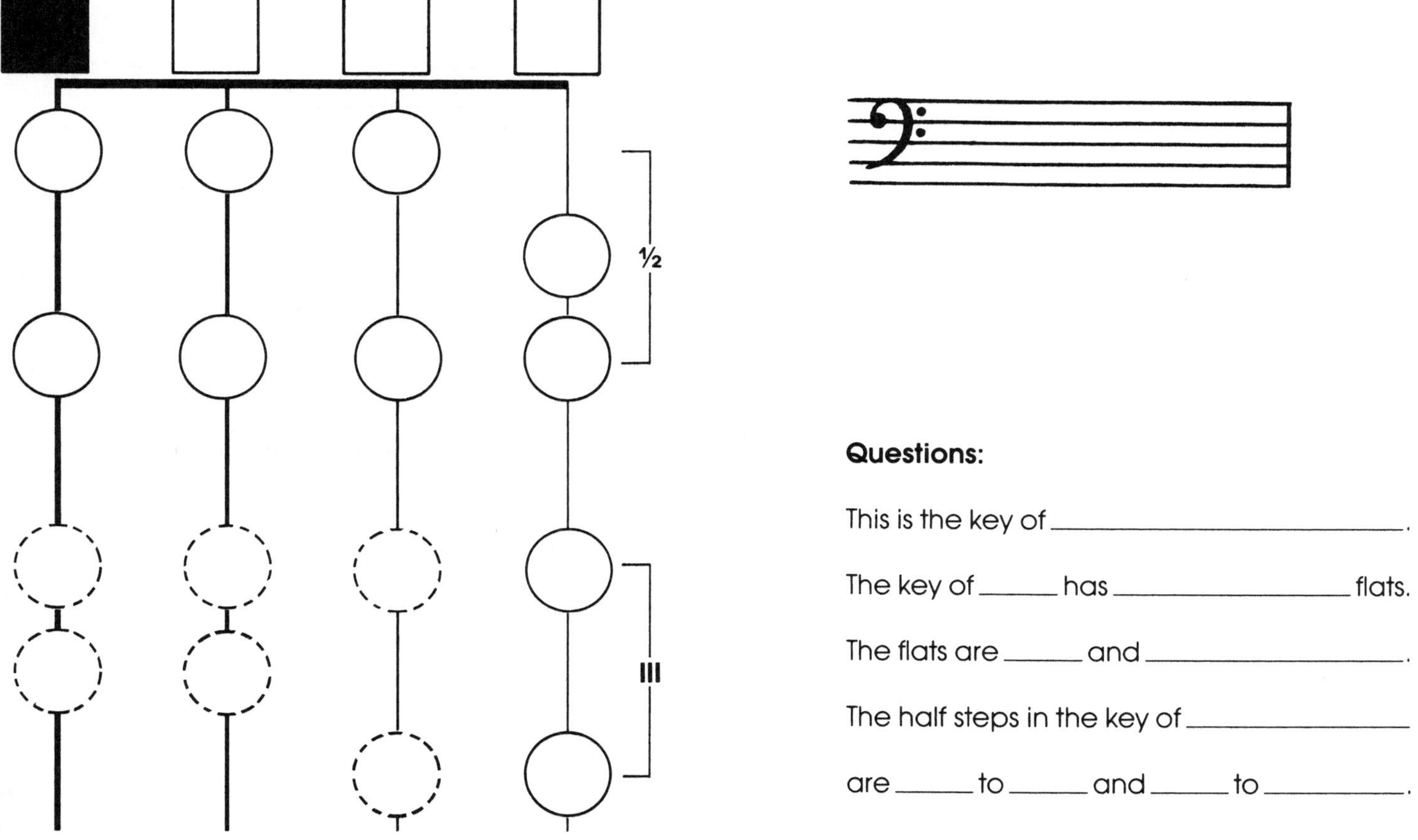

Questions:

This is the key of ________________________.

The key of ______ has ________________ flats.

The flats are ______ and ________________.

The half steps in the key of ________________

are ______ to ______ and ______ to __________.

92. DRAW NOTES/NAME NOTES

Draw a note on the staff for each note shown in the fingering chart above. (low to high) Use whole notes.
Name the notes on the blanks provided, add the key signature, and place half step markings where
appropriate.

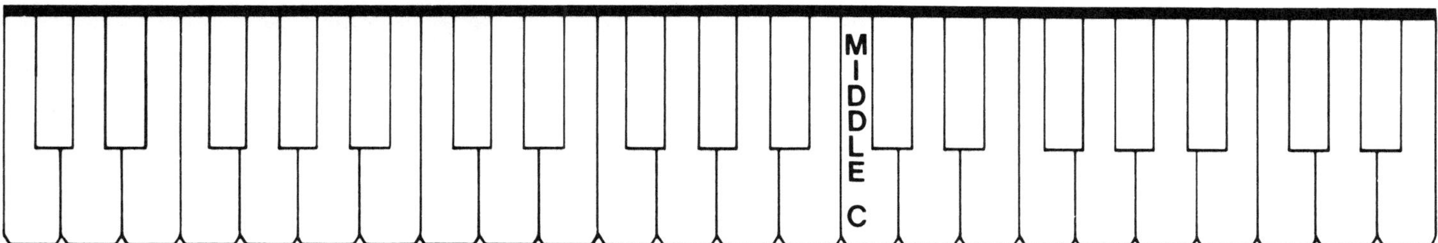

93. KEYBOARD STUDY

Write the letters on the keys for the one octave B♭ Major scale. Show proper relationship to middle C.

94. DEFINE TERMS AND SIGNS

Define the following or state what the word or sign wants you to do.

1. Accent ____

2. Arpeggio ____

3. Chromatic ____

4. Common Time _____________________________________

5. Crescendo ____

6. ₵ ____

7. Détaché ____

8. Diminuendo ______________________________________

9. Double Stop ______________________________________

10. Duet ____

11. Dynamics ____

12. Etude ____

13. Flat ____

14. Interval ____

15. Major Scale _____________________________________

16. Melodic Minor Scale ______________________________

17. ♩ ____

18. Round ____

19. Staccato ____

20. Simile ____

21. Tempo ____

22. Theme ____

23. Triplet ____

24. Tuning ____

25. Vibrato ____